The Beaver Book of Games

Ball games, chasing games, card, party and word games, tricks and stunts are just some of the items in the *Beaver Book of Games*. Old favourites such as Rounders, Draughts and Skittles are included, together with variations on games and lots of new ones. George and Cornelia Kay have travelled widely and introduce some games from overseas in this collection, which will give children of all ages plenty of ideas for indoor and outdoor activities.

The Beaver Book of

for indoors and outdoors

George and Cornelia Kay

Illustrated by Robin Anderson

Beaver Books

First published in 1977 by
The Hamlyn Publishing Group Limited
London · New York · Sydney · Toronto
Astronaut House, Feltham, Middlesex, England

ISBN 0 600 34033 3

Printed in England by Cox & Wyman Limited
London, Reading and Fakenham
Set in Monotype Garamond

Contents

PLAY THE GAME

Do you sometimes get bored with watching TV or listening to radio and records? There's no need for that, is there? There's always some fascinating hobby you can adopt or a new and welcome game you can play.

Of course, you probably already know and play lots of games. In your school or youth organisation you most likely play team games such as soccer, cricket, tennis and hockey. Those games are deservedly popular. The trouble is that they require special play areas, enough numbers to make up teams, and the equipment can be expensive.

That's why we hope you will find this book interesting and useful. There are simple games and difficult games, games to play by yourself, with one opponent, or with a crowd of friends. Some will help to brighten up dull days when you are indoors, or make your party a red-letter event. Others will give you bright ideas for outdoor fun. For almost all of the games the simple equipment you need will already be lying around at home. Just a few of the games will require the spending of a few pence or some easy do-it-yourself preparation.

You may find that you know a number of these games quite well, but play them under different rules. The difference hardly matters, because the games are just as much fun either way. There's no need to take them too seriously, though it's always good to win!

Turn the pages and pick out a few games to try today. There will still be plenty of ideas left for another day, and many, many days after that.

OUTDOOR GAMES

Ball Games

Dodge Ball

You need ten or more players for this game. The ball should be large and fairly soft. An inflatable beach ball is fine, but don't inflate it too hard.

All players but one form as large a circle as possible. The remaining player, the Dodger, stands in the centre of the circle. On the word 'go', the player in the ring who has the ball throws it, trying to hit the Dodger, who can move within the circle as much as he likes to avoid being hit.

The players forming the ring must not move their feet, and the only hit which is successful, enabling the thrower to exchange his place with the Dodger, is below the waist.

If the ball fails to hit the Dodger it is picked up and thrown again by anyone in the ring who can reach it. If no one can, the Dodger picks up the ball and throws it to any player he likes to restart the game.

The faster the game is played the more enjoyable it is, so players in the ring must be ready to catch a ball which misses its target and rapidly get rid of it in another attempt to hit the Dodger.

Rounders

You have probably played your own version of rounders, which is a very old English game. It was taken to the New World by pioneers following in the wake of the Pilgrim Fathers, and gradually developed into America's national game, baseball.

Nearly a hundred years ago British enthusiasts for the old English game drew up some rules, and you may like to play rounders as it really should be played.

The space needed for the game does not have to be very large, but the five bases, marked by stones or small sticks as shown in diagram A, should ideally be about twelve metres apart.

There should be two teams of nine players for two innings. If you only have five players in a team (the smallest number for a good game) the number of bases can be reduced to four, spaced as shown in diagram B.

Another stone or stick marks the pitcher's base (see both diagrams).

The first batsman (holding a very small cricket bat or a cut-down broom handle) stands at base 1 (or 'home') with the rest of the team in a row well behind him. The opposing team, apart from one member selected as a pitcher, stands around outside the bases as fielders.

The ball – a cricket ball or any kind which does not bounce too much – is bowled underarm to reach the batsman between head and knees, without bouncing first. You decide before starting the game how many balls may be bowled at each batsman, but four is usual.

The batsman can refuse any ball he does not like, but he must run if he uses his bat, whether he hits the ball or not, and of course with the last ball he must run in any case.

After hitting the ball, the batsman drops the bat and runs as far as he can round the pitch, passing all the bases in

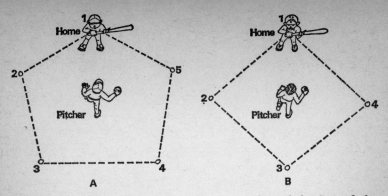

A   B

numerical order. If he succeeds in running right round, he has scored one 'rounder'. He picks up the bat and has another turn. If he does not make a complete round he remains on the base he reaches and the second member of the team takes up the bat. Only one player can stand on any one base, so those already on bases must move ahead when they see the batsman starting to run.

A batsman is out if caught off a hit ball; if a fielder, ball in hand, touches a base before the batsman can reach it; if the batsman is touched by a fielder, ball in hand, between posts; and if he is touched by a fielder, ball in hand, while still at the batting post after trying to hit a fair ball. When a batsman is out, any other player on a base remains there till there are no other players left to bat.

The game is won by the team that gets the greatest number of players back to the first base without being out.

French Cricket

There is no need to give an elaborate description of this garden game, just a few rules so as to avoid arguments. The ball, whether hard or soft, should not be so bouncy that a strong hit will sent it out of the garden or through a window. The bat should be small – a toy cricket bat rather than a standard one, or just a cricket stump or rounded pole of the same thickness and length. Bowling must always be under-arm. A hit on the batsman does not count if it is above the batsman's knee.

It is a 'no ball' if the player who reaches the hit ball moves his feet after touching it, and if two or more fielders touch each other when competing to reach the ball.

You can organise scoring if you like. Agree beforehand on scores for boundaries – two for a ball hit beyond the side of the lawn, four if it goes beyond either end of the lawn, and so on. A batsman also gets one point for each 'no ball' played to him.

A batsman is out if he moves his feet (he can face in any direction he chooses at the start of his innings), if the ball hits his leg below the knee, or if a hit ball is caught by any other player before it touches the ground.

Bounce in the Pail

You may have seen a version of this game on fairgrounds, and realise that it is more difficult than it looks.

Take a plastic or metal household pail – it should be about twenty-five centimetres deep and of a similar diameter – and prop it up on one side with soil, sand or stones so that it stands tilted slightly towards you. The lowest point of the rim should be about twelve centimetres from the ground.

Mark a throwing line two metres from the pail.

Each player has three chances to bounce a ball on the ground in front of the pail so that the ball enters the pail and remains inside. Tennis balls are best, but any ball of a similar size with plenty of bounce will serve just as well.

If you play this game indoors prop the tilted pail with a few books. Use table tennis balls thrown directly into the pail, and not bounced first.

Stoolball

Some people believe that this very old game was the ancestor of cricket. It was almost forgotten after cricket became popular. Then a doctor thought it would be splendid exercise for First World War soldiers recovering from injuries. Anyway, it is a good game to play in a garden or yard as a change from cricket because there is no real need to have eleven on each side and not much space is required.

You will need to get two pieces of hardboard thirty centimetres square and nail them at the top of two posts long enough to project 1·4 metres above the ground after they have been fairly firmly fixed in a hole. The posts need

not be very thick, and in softwood they are quite cheap.

The poles should be fixed 14·5 metres apart, one at each end of the pitch, with the boards facing each other. Don't worry too much about the length of the pitch – just as close to the above length as space allows.

Use a table tennis bat and a soft rubber ball for play. The batsman stands in front of one of the poles. The bowler must throw underarm, and the ball must not bounce before hitting the board or being hit by the batsman. Fielders can stand anywhere around the pitch. The batsman is out if the ball hits the board behind him or is caught after he has hit it, if he is run out, if the ball hits any part of his body or if he hits the ball twice before it touches the ground.

Runs are scored by hitting across the boundary (decide on one, two or four runs according to the size of the play area) or by running to the other post.

If you have several players you can, of course, have batsmen at both ends. Ten balls make an over.

Some old pictures show this game being played without a bat, the soft ball being hit with the open hand. It is quite a good idea because the ball is not hit so far, spoiling flower beds or going over the neighbour's fence. But in this hand-play be sure that the ball is a really soft one!

Aerial Tennis

We first saw this game being played in San Francisco, and were told it is popular all over the United States, so it is strange that few people in Europe know about it. When we have explained it to young friends it has caught on in a big way, as an easier version of badminton.

You need a fairly large space of lawn or yard. The same

size as a tennis court is ideal, but you can easily adapt a smaller area. Perhaps the best place of all is a stretch of level sand at the seaside when the tide goes out, because there it is easy to mark out the lines of the court.

Play is with table tennis bats and a shuttlecock, and one, two or three people can play on each side. String a line between two bamboos or any fences or trees so that the line hangs two metres from the ground. Whatever size of court you can manage, a service line should be marked three metres from the line 'net' on each side. The server, who tosses the shuttlecock in the air and hits it over the 'net', must not stand inside the area marked by the service line.

The server has only one chance to get the shuttlecock over the 'net'. Players may not hit the shuttlecock more than once to return it successfully, nor let it touch the ground. And, of course, you lose if you fail to return it or hit it outside the court.

Scoring can be as in tennis or table tennis, but table tennis scoring is simpler. That is, five services for each side in turn until one side has scored twenty-one. As aerial tennis is a very active game, with a lot of running about, you can ignore the table tennis rule about players who reach twenty-all taking alternate services until one gets a two points lead, and instead the first to reach twenty-one brings the game to an end.

Crockey

This game, which is similar to golf, can be played solo or with as many friends as you wish.

On a piece of paper draw a rough plan of your proposed

course, starting at one corner and marking the 'holes' as haphazardly as you wish and as far apart as possible. You should try to have at least nine holes, which you then mark in a lawn with a small stick driven into the ground, or on a hard surface with a stone about three centimetres at its widest point. Number the sticks or stones from 1 to 9.

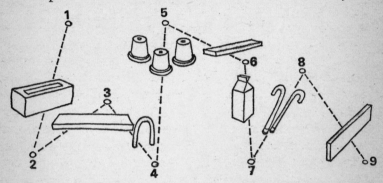

Next mark out on your plan the rough position of your 'bunkers'. These can be old bricks, boxes, pairs of sticks laid flat to make a narrow passage, and a few pieces of wood, about five centimetres high when laid flat, to act as barriers. The sketch here gives you one idea for your layout. You can think of many more ingenious and baffling obstacles.

All you need to play is a hockey stick, a golf club, or a walking-stick and a lemon. As a real lemon is expensive and will get bruised, wait until Mum has an empty plastic lemon, which you can then fill with water.

The game is played just as in golf, driving off from the starting 'tee' in the corner towards the first 'hole', which must be touched by the lemon and then driven from that point without being handled to the next 'hole', avoiding all the obstacles on the way.

The number of strokes needed to complete the course are counted, and the player who goes round with the lowest number of hits is the winner.

Chasing Games

Scorpion Sting

As you may know, scorpions can inflict a nasty sting from the rear just as wasps and bees do. Every child in Asia knows how painful such stings can be, and that is why this make-believe game is popular all over the East.

The more players the better, but you can manage quite well with four or five friends. The play zone should not be too large, say three metres wide and four metres in length unless you have many players, when almost any large size will be all right.

One player is chosen as scorpion and crawls about on all fours. The other players move around the play zone, avoiding the crawling scorpion but daring themselves to touch the scorpion's head.

That could be easy enough, but for the fact that the scorpion can sting anyone who comes within range of his legs. If he touches anyone with his foot, which, of course, he can do only sideways or to the rear as he must keep his hands on the ground, the scorpion changes place with his victim.

It is best to play this game on grass, or the scorpion may graze his hands. And you have probably realized that you can play Scorpion Sting indoors if the furniture is moved from the centre of a fairly large room.

Indian Tag

All but two of the players pair off and stand with hands on hips and one arm linked through their partner's arm. The two remaining players are the Rajah and Servant.

In preparation for the chase the paired players, the Rajah and the Servant scatter. On the word 'go' the Rajah chases after the Servant. The Servant can find safety simply by linking his arm through one of the unlinked arms of a pair, the other member of the pair then having to withdraw his arm, becoming the chased Servant.

Naturally the pairs do their best to avoid getting near the running Servant, while he has both to find a pair which cannot elude him and to evade the pursuing Rajah.

When a Rajah catches the Servant, the two change places and the game is resumed.

Hoppity

There should be eight or more players for this chasing game.

All but one of the players stand in as wide a circle as space allows, facing towards the centre. The extra player stands in the centre.

On the word 'go' he hops outside the ring and continues hopping past them in a clockwise direction, suddenly touching one of them on the shoulder. The player thus touched immediately hops as close as he can get to the other player, and both continue hopping in a clockwise direction on the outside of the ring in a race to see who first can reach the vacant space.

The hopper who first reaches the vacant spot is safe, and the other moves to the centre in readiness for another turn.

Release

This is a wonderful game if you can assemble two teams of at least ten players in each team, and if you can play in the countryside with plenty of trees and bushes, or there is a big, wide beach at your holiday resort, again with hiding places among the rocks and breakwaters.

You can also play Release quite well if there are pedestrian areas connecting blocks of flats. But whatever you do, wherever you decide to play it, be sure the area is free from all traffic because everyone will be running fast and dodging hither and thither.

After the two teams have been selected and agreement reached on the hunting area (there should be sensible boundaries beyond which no one is allowed), one team scatters. The other team closes its eyes and counts up to 100. This team is gathered round home – a tree, rock, post, or other sizeable object which can be touched at shoulder height.

After the count is over the hunting team scatters in search of the other team, the members of which keep on the move to avoid being seen, or if seen, to avoid being caught.

Capture is achieved by grabbing a quarry and patting him three times on the back (any other part of the body doesn't count). When this happens the quarry admits capture and is led back to the home post. He is left there, with his promise to keep one hand on the home post.

As more prisoners are brought in they join hands to make a human chain, the first prisoner still keeping one hand on the post. Providing this chain remains connected to the home post in this way, the prisoners can swing round at the head of the line as much as the last prisoner wishes in the hopes of an ally releasing them.

After one or two prisoners have been taken the members of the team still free have to try to rescue their friends. This is done by rushing in and touching the player at the head of the chain, whereupon all are freed and can scatter to safety.

Naturally the capturing team keeps the best watch possible over their prisoners, but guards can be tempted away by the sighting of a player still uncaptured. Then another player can, with luck and speed, rush in to release his team mates.

There is an important rule about capture. Only one player may take his prisoner with the three taps on the back. If a team-mate of the captor comes too close, and the struggling prisoner (probably lying on his back to avoid those hand pats) can reach out with hands or feet and just touch the second man he must be allowed to go free.

A short bout of playing this rather rough but very exciting game will show that speed and cunning are important for both sides. The ability to fall flat on your back and stay that way helps to avoid capture, and strength in forcing someone to expose his back for the necessary three taps is an asset for the capturing side.

So you need to wear old clothes for the game and must not worry about a bruise or two! It is certainly not a game for the very young, but fine for anyone who enjoys the rough and tumble of, say, a game of football.

Snake Chase

Plenty of room is needed for this game, so it is ideal if you are at the seaside or in some open space in the country. And it really needs at least a dozen players.

One is chosen as 'he'. The others scatter within an agreed area – anywhere beyond it being out of bounds. After closing his eyes and counting up to fifty 'he' starts searching for, and chasing, his quarry.

The slightest touch means capture, and the captive goes behind 'he', placing his hands on 'he's' shoulders.

The chase continues, each captive joining the growing snake. Although only 'he' at the head can use his hands, any player who becomes part of the snake can help to make a capture by touching a player with his foot, elbow or any part of his body, as long as he does not lift his hands from the shoulders of the person in front of him.

To make the game exciting the free players do not just hide away but dare themselves to tease the snake by running close to it and then darting away. As the snake becomes longer the daring player has to be very careful that the snake's tail does not suddenly curve round while he is watching for danger from the head.

Tierce

The name of this game comes from an old French word introduced to England by the Norman soldiers under William the Conqueror. It means 'three', and you can see that it is a very old game, but none the worse for that.

The more players you have the better, but there must be an even number, say ten, twelve or fourteen. All but two of the players stand in pairs, one member of the pair behind the other, facing into the centre of as wide a circle as space allows. One of the two special players is named as 'he' and stands in the centre. The other player, chosen as the Tierce, goes behind the circle of paired players and strolls around, waiting for the word 'go'.

On the signal the Tierce runs either way round the circle, changing direction as often as he wishes, with 'he' doing his best to keep close to him. 'He' must not leave the circle, and Tierce must not come inside it – until he sees the chance to dash in and stand in front of a pair before 'he' touches him.

Immediately Tierce turns a pair into a group of three the player at the rear becomes Tierce and starts running outside the circle, looking for a chance to dash in and stand in front of a pair.

When 'he' successfully touches Tierce before the latter is standing still in front of a pair, Tierce enters the circle and becomes 'he', while the original 'he' runs to any pair he chooses, stands in front of it, and thus turns the player at the rear into the new Tierce.

There are no winners in this game. It just goes on until you are tired out.

Rodeo Round-up

A fairly large space is needed for the round-up, but it must have a definite boundary, such as the edges of a lawn or the lines on a playing pitch. Neither cowboys nor wild horses may go beyond the boundary.

At least twelve players are needed, and up to twenty are much better. By tossing a coin decide who will be cowboys plus horses, and who will be wild horses. The simplest method is to regard 'heads' as the former and 'tails' the latter, with any odd player among the 'heads' joining the 'tails'.

The 'heads' pair off, each pair deciding who shall be the rider and who the horse. The lighter of the pair should be

the rider because he has to mount piggy-back on the other.

On the word 'go', the pairs begin chasing the wild horses (those whose coin came down 'tails'). Pairs can chase on their own or co-operate to corner a wild horse, but the rider must firmly touch some part of the wild horse with his arm, shoulder or body without falling off his mount.

Once touched, the wild horse must admit capture and not run off. He is led to the side of the arena and the chase is continued after the wild horses still free.

Contests

Hit the Penny

If you ever go to South America you will see children playing this game in the parks and playgrounds.

Drive a thin post – part of a broomstick is fine so long as you get someone to cut the top flat and level – into the ground so that the post is about thirty centimetres high.

Scratch or chalk a circle one metre in diameter round the post. Players stand in a circle so that no one is less than two metres from the post. If you can manage it, mark this larger circle too. On top of the post a coin (a 1p or a 2p piece for example) is lodged.

Each player gets five turns with a small round pebble (a hard, solid rubber ball is better) and must try to knock the coin off the post. Each time the coin falls inside the small ring he gains one point. Each time the coin flies beyond the ring he gets five points.

You can agree beforehand that each player has one throw in turn, but it makes it easier to keep everyone's score if all five turns are taken at once by each player.

Marbles

Alleys, taws, bools – these are some of the names for marbles. There are scores of others in every language, for marble games have been played in ancient Egypt, Rome and China ever since children enjoyed games; and not only children – adults have nearly always been as keen as anyone else, with rich people in 18th century England having sets of the tiny balls carved from real marble, hence the modern name.

The **Simple** game is for two or more players. One rolls his marble by flicking it into the chosen playing area, which should be fairly level. There are two ways of flicking. The first is to rest the marble on the underneath of the forefinger and middle finger held together and flick it off with the thumb. The second method is to hold the marble between the top of the thumb and the inner side of the forefinger, then flicking the thumb.

After the first player's marble has come to rest his opponent flicks his marble in an attempt to hit the first marble. If he succeeds he picks up both. If he fails, the first player flicks another marble at his opponent's. If he hits it he picks up all three marbles. If he fails there are three marbles to win. The game thus proceeds until one player has won all his opponent's marbles.

For the **Circle** game draw a rough chalk circle about one metre in diameter on a tarmac or concrete surface. Each player (it is best to have at least four for this game) puts one marble anywhere he chooses inside the circle. From an agreed starting point each player flicks a marble in an attempt to knock one or more of the marbles. He wins any marbles thus knocked out of the circle and has another go, but if he fails to knock a marble out of the circle the next player has a turn.

The flicked marble is left in the circle if it comes to rest there. If it rolls outside the circle that is the flicking position for the player's next turn, using that marble again.

The Fort is a marble scoring game. Three circles are drawn, one inside the other. The largest circle should be one metre in diameter, the next half a metre, and the innermost one fifteen centimetres. A flicking line (which must be straight) is drawn at a distance of about two metres from the largest circle.

Each player has five marbles, and each set of five should be of a different colour, so that players can easily identify their own marbles at the end of the game.

A marble coming to rest in the outside ring scores one point, in the next ring five points, and in the innermost ring ten points, but the score is not taken until all the players have shot all their marbles.

Apart from flicking one's own marbles into the highest scoring ring, the object is to knock opponents' marbles out of that ring, or outside the rings altogether, when, of course, they score nothing.

Breaking the Ring needs at least four players. Draw a large circle, at least two metres in diameter. The flicking line is drawn two metres from the edge of the circle.

Each player places two of his marbles somewhere on the rim of the circle, placing them wherever he wishes but, for his own advantage, making the space between the marbles as great as possible.

Each player has a marble called a shooter, which is used at every turn. If you can obtain a larger marble for the shooter it helps identification.

Each player in turn flicks his shooter marble into the circle and tries to knock one of the marbles lying on the ring's edge *outside* the circle. If he succeeds he then keeps it as his win. If he fails to knock a marble outside the ring, either missing altogether or merely shifting a marble inside the ring, he must add another marble to the rim. Whether

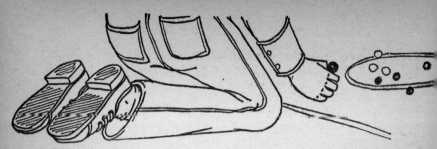

he wins or loses on his turn, he retrieves his shooter for the next attempt.

Marbles knocked inside the rim and then, on a subsequent turn, knocked by accident outside the ring, are placed to one side. The player who knocks the last marble on the rim outside the circle also wins all the marbles taken out of the play and placed in reserve.

Before the game begins there should be agreement on how many marbles each player should have for placing on the rim. To keep the game going they should have at least six each. Anyone with no more marbles to place on the rim drops out of the game.

Gateways is played on a smooth, hard surface with a wall or a large piece of timber at the edge. Against this wall lay five bricks on their long sides, with the spaces between them varying as follows: ten centimetres between the first and second bricks, five centimetres between the second and third, ten centimetres between the third and fourth.

Marbles are flicked from a line at least three metres from the bricks. Any marble landing in the left or right hand space and not bouncing out again scores one; any marble in the centre space scores five.

You can increase the number of bricks and spaces if you have a sufficiently wide playing area, varying the width of the spaces, and following the rule that the narrower the space, the higher the score.

If you have no bricks handy any block of wood or rectangular object fifteen to twenty centimetres in length will serve equally well.

Jumping the River

A simple game for the younger guests at a party. Place two long bamboo sticks on the ground about half a metre apart. See that there is plenty of space for a run before the sticks and room to go beyond them without mishap. Explain that the bamboos represent the banks of a river which is beginning to flood, and the players must jump to the opposite bank. Widen the distance between the bamboos after each round until all but one intrepid traveller has failed to jump across.

Skittles

If you would like to play skittles much as it was when travellers brought it back from Europe in the days of the Black Prince (it was then called Kails) you need to find a flat and level space for your alley, about seven metres long and a metre wide.

The pins, as the target objects are called, used to be made from heavy wood, carved roughly in the shape of a bottle, and standing thirty centimetres high. Nine of these pins were placed at the end of the alley in three rows to form a square, with one corner pointing towards the other end, and the pins about ten centimetres apart. The missile used was a disc-shaped piece of wood rather like a thick plate. If you can play with a circular wooden bread board that would be fine. But a cricket ball will be quite all right, though it makes the game somewhat easier because a perfectly round ball will continue straight while a disc or flattened ball is liable to curve away at the end of its run.

Scoring is as follows: three points if you knock all the pins over with one throw; two points if all are knocked over after two throws, one point if all are knocked over after three throws. No score if after three throws one or more pins remain standing.

This is the hardest version of the game. You may prefer, at first, to let each player have three throws in a row, rearranging the skittles after each throw, and score one point for every pin knocked over. Thus the maximum score for any player in this game is twenty-seven points.

What can you use as pins? The unbreakable and non-returnable glass bottles in which drinks like ginger ale, bitter lemon and tonic water are sold will be fine. Empty soft drinks cans will do as a second choice, but if you use them make the square rather smaller than suggested above. This is because they are not as likely to fall over and knock each other down as real wooden pins or soft drinks bottles.

Whatever you do, don't be tempted to make do with breakable bottles. Broken glass is very dangerous even to pick up gently, and you are bound to leave some splinters which would injure you or someone else playing in the same place days later.

Flicks

Long, long ago, when your grandparents were your age and picture cards were given away with cigarettes, packets of tea, and even chocolate bars, this was a winning and losing game popular in every playground and open space so long as it had a wall or fence.

You can play Flicks with playing cards, even though there will not be the thrill of speculating with your own collection and winning those of your friends, and you have to give them back to the owner of the pack at the end.

The game is simple enough. Stand one card against the wall, its base a little way from the wall so that the card will remain nearly vertical. Players, each with the same number of cards, stand, kneel or crouch beyond on an agreed line from the wall, say two metres.

Each player, in turn, holding a card between the first and second fingers of his hand, throws or flicks it at the target card and tries to knock it down. There is not much point in doing so at the first shot in the game, for all that happens is that the successful player retrieves his own card, sets up the target card, and has another turn. But after unsuccessful flicks, when a number of cards are lying around the target card, the player who knocks the target card down wins all the cards lying around it, and the number can be large.

There can be as many players as you wish, from two up-wards. But everyone should have at least ten cards to start, so with more than five players two packs of playing cards are needed.

Jacks

This is another very old game played all over the world under many different names, including Five Stones or Six Stones in many parts of Britain. There are dozens of versions. Here we give three of the most popular.

You need to collect five or six small pebbles for each player – not too round or they will roll too far – and a rubber ball with good bouncing qualities. The game is played on any hard surface. You can play it by yourself or with as many opponents as you wish.

With water paints or a felt pen number your pebbles, marking both sides so that the number can be seen which-ever way the pebble falls.

Holding five pebbles in one hand and the ball in the other, the player gently scatters the pebbles in front of him. Then he tosses the ball in the air, bends down from a standing position and picks up pebble 1 with the same hand before the ball bounces, and catches the ball after it has bounced once. He can transfer the pebble from his ball-catching hand to the other one before or after he catches the ball, but the pebble must not be in his throwing hand when he tosses the ball a second time.

He then bends down and picks up pebble 2, catching the ball after the bounce, and continues in this way until he has all five pebbles in his hand. Dropping a pebble, failing to pick up the right one, or missing the ball after it bounces means he is out of the game. He then clears any remaining pebbles out of the way. The next player scatters his pebbles and begins the ball-tossing and pebble-collecting routine.

Another and harder version, needing six pebbles, is to collect the pebbles in increasing numbers each time – 1 on the first ball, 2 and 3 on the second throw, 4, 5 and 6 on the last ball. This is a quicker game but much more difficult.

A third version (and here you have to toss the ball as high as you can to give you time for the collecting) is to collect the pebbles one at a time and in their numerical order, as in the first game described, but before the ball bounces you must pick up the right pebble and place it in a 'nest', which is a circle about fifteen centimetres in diameter drawn on the ground beside the player.

The winner in any of these games is the first player to complete the game without making a mistake.

Traffic Signals

This is today's version of the old game known as Creepers or Catch-Me-Moving. Choose as large a space as you can – at least four metres wide and ten metres long.

Players are divided into two teams, with one player as the traffic controller. He stands at the far end of the area with his back to the other players. The members of the two teams gather in two single files at the opposite end, ready to move up the two imaginary roads along each side of the space.

The game starts with the controller shouting 'green', whereupon all the drivers begin hopping towards him. Then he suddenly calls 'amber' and all drivers must proceed with caution, by moving on all fours.

Immediately after calling 'amber', the controller turns

round and points to one side or the other while shouting 'red'. All the players on that side must freeze into position and not move. He can then, if he wishes, call 'red' to the side still moving on all fours, or he can turn back again, calling 'amber', followed either by 'green' (without turning) or 'red', again quickly turning and pointing.

Anyone not on all fours when the controller calls 'amber' just before he turns, or anyone he catches moving after his red signal, falls out.

The controller must follow the correct signal sequence of green-amber-red and red-amber-green, but he can vary the period of each colour just as he wishes.

All the motorists are very unskilled! They may bump into each other, and anyone compelled to use both legs while hopping or knocked over when crawling must go back to the start.

The winner is the first motorist to reach the edge of the area beside the controller without being caught disobeying the signals. He becomes controller for the next drive.

Hopscotch

If you lived in a French town you would call this game *Pierres*. If you are Scottish you will have changed this French word for stones to Peevers. In the rest of the English-speaking world town children accept that they have copied the Scottish game, hence the second part of the word Hopscotch.

All you need is a flat, smooth surface, a piece of chalk to draw a pattern on the gound, and a small flat pebble for each player.

There are very many patterns to draw, and you can make

up your own design, or just follow the lines made by paving stones or crazy paving in the garden (in the latter case play will be difficult if the pieces of paving are very small).

The sketch shows a popular design called the pillar box. Other good ones are the aircraft, the ladder, and the train. All you need is to draw a rough outline of the object chosen and then to divide it into separate sections. There should always be nine of these 'beds', as they are called, and they should be numbered as shown in the sketch.

If you are asked to play with someone who already knows about Hopscotch you will be told of the rules accepted by his friends. These rules will probably be different from the ideas we give here, as there are almost as many versions of the game as there are towns where it is played. But our description will give you the basic idea.

A player stands close to the bottom edge of the pattern and tosses his pebble into bed 1. If the pebble does not touch any line and is in the correct bed the player hops into that bed in one movement, bends down, still on one foot, picks up his pebble, and hops out again to the throwing place.

Provided he has not overbalanced or allowed his foot to touch a line he then tosses his pebble into bed 2, hops into bed 1 and then to bed 2, picking up his pebble and returning in the same way, and so on until he reaches bed 9 and hops to 'Out'. If you look at the diagram, you will see that 5 and 6 are a bit tricky!

When he fails to toss the pebble correctly or hop in and out without a mistake, he stands aside and the next player has his turn.

After all players have had a turn, the first player starts the next round, tossing his pebble into the bed where he failed in the previous round.

One very popular extra to this basic game is that each player leaves his pebble in the last bed he successfully reached, hopping to that bed when he has his turn in the next round and resuming the game from there, still standing on one leg.

In the meantime, the bed occupied by a pebble is regarded as 'taken', and other players need not toss their pebble into it. When retrieving their pebble from a bed with a higher number, they must hop over the occupied bed.

To explain by an example. John's pebble touches a line when he tries to toss it into bed 4. He hops to the pebble and places it in bed 3, his last successful bedding. Chris, who has already tossed and hopped into beds 1 and 2, need not worry about bed 3, now occupied, but tosses his pebble into bed 4. But when he hops to retrieve his pebble from bed 4 he must hop from bed 2 to bed 4, missing the occupied bed 3.

Quoits

There is no law nowadays to prevent you playing this game, though hundreds of years ago it was banned in England. This was because the king believed boys and men were playing quoits instead of practising with bows and arrows, and worried that the famous bowmen of England would not in future be as skilled as they had been at the battles of Agincourt and Crécy.

Officially the quoit should be a metal ring not more than twenty-one centimetres in diameter and weighing about three kilograms, thrown into a circle one metre in diametre. There should be two of these circles, with a short upright metal pin marking each centre. The pins are knocked into the ground 16·5 metres apart. Those are the

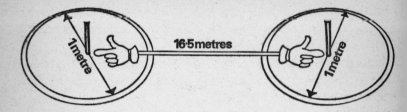

16·5metres

1 metre

1 metre

details if you ever want to play the old English game. See the sketch above.

It will be much simpler to prepare the game on a smaller scale. You will need two or three rubber rings for each player – the kind sold for beach and garden games. They should be about ten centimetres in diameter on the inner side.

Take two pieces of wood – bamboo is good – to serve as the pins. Press these into the grass four to five metres apart, so that only about three centimetres are above ground. Now take a piece of string and an old paint brush, tying one end of the string to the brush and the other end to the pin stuck in the ground.

The length between brush and pin should be about twenty-five centimetres. Dip the brush into the white fluid sold for marking games pitches (it won't hurt the grass) and, with the string held taut, mark out a circle, first round one pin and then round the other.

The players take turns to stand inside one circle and aim their quoits at the pin in the other, throwing all their quoits at once. One point is scored by the thrower whose quoit is nearest the pin and two for a quoit over the pin (known as a ringer).

No points are gained if opponents' quoits are the same distance from the pin or if two are over it.

After the first round of throws, players pick up their quoits and throw into the circle where they first stood, the changeover continuing until one player has scored eleven points which ends the game.

As you may have seen in some films, in America the game is often played with horseshoes and if you can get small worn shoes from ponies these make a better game than the rubber rings, as it is more difficult to get them to stay over the pin.

Races

Balancing Race

Unless the play area is very wide this race is best run in a
series of heats with not more than two or three entrants each
time. The track should be at least fifteen metres long, and
the race is there and back, so some kind of starting and
finishing lines is needed.

Entrants stand with arms stretched out sideways, palms
downwards. Someone places a coin or counter on the back
of each hand and then calls out 'ready, steady, go'.

The race is up to the far line, with the space beyond it
touched by both feet, and then back to the starting line.

Anyone dropping a coin or counter must pick it up
and go back to the starting line to try again – unless his
rival has already completed the course.

If you want to make this race even more difficult use
small potatoes or pebbles instead of counters or coins.

Ralegh's Race

You all know the story about Sir Walter Ralegh (that is
how he spelt his name, whatever your history book says!)

gallantly placing his cloak on a muddy patch so that his Queen did not get mud on her shoes. Presumably the puddle was small and one step took Elizabeth I to dry ground. In this race the wet patch is as large as your lawn or playground.

Pair off the players, a boy and a girl in each pair if you can. The object is for each boy to conduct his girl partner dry-footed from one end of the area to the other more quickly than the other couples.

Each boy is given two small articles of old clothing – dusters, pieces of towelling, and similar articles will do – and he moves them one at a time for the girl's feet. She in her turn must not allow her feet to touch the ground beyond the material and of course she must not overbalance. If either mishap occurs the couple returns to the starting line and tries again.

Crazy Relay

For a small area in which an ordinary relay race would be over too quickly a crazy relay is a good idea. Mark out a roughly circular route with a few posts or stones so that there is a track at least a metre wide.

Divide the entrants into two or three teams of five or more in each team. In a relay race the members of the team take turns at covering the track, so that the second person takes over when the first person gets back to base, and is in turn followed by the third member of the team. In a crazy relay, each stretch requires a different kind of race, so you need five ideas if there are five in a team, for example.

Here are some ideas for each stretch, which someone should write down so that he can explain what is to be done before the race starts.

Hopping. All fours. Backwards. Sideways. Three-legged with the runner on the previous stretch. Sack race. Potato on a spoon. Wheelbarrow with the runner on the previous stretch. Blindfold.

Backwards on All Fours

A very simple race to run on the lawn or any grassy surface which is large enough to provide a course at least fifteen metres long.

Racers line up at the starting end with their backs to the winning line. On the word 'go' they drop down on all fours, hands and feet touching the ground, and start moving. Neither knees nor elbows must touch the ground and bumping is not permitted. Anyone breaking these rules is scratched from the race.

It sound easy, but it is hard to keep straight, to avoid bumping into anyone and at the same time to move faster than the other entrants.

Fruit Race

You need a fairly level area for this race, providing a track about six metres long and wide enough to allow half a metre between competitors, who are divided into two teams but all run together. If four are competing against four you will therefore require a width of about four metres.

At each end of the double tracks place some object as a marker, and give each runner a teaspoon and an apple, lemon or potato.

Controlling the fruit only with the teaspoon, runners roll the fruit down the course, round the marker and back to the starting point, one runner becoming the overall winner as well as team winner, with another runner, either in the winner's team or the winner in the second group, being judged second.

If you want a longer game, play it as a relay, with only one fruit for each team, the members taking over in turn as the fruit is successfully rolled up and back.

Pushing and jostling by rival runners (watch for trouble at the turns!) are forbidden. The guilty runner has to drop out of the race. If it is being run as a relay the team-mate of the offending player must retrieve the fruit and re-run the stretch on which the offence took place in one direction, as well as running his own part of the race.

INDOOR GAMES

Board and Table Games

Darts

One thing about the game of darts – and we hope it does not put you off – is that playing it will rapidly turn you into a mathematician. You quickly learn to subtract and multiply like a computer.

There is no point in describing the dimensions of a dart board, for any good board you buy will be of a standard size. The darts are also made to an exact size. Remember that the point is sharp and the dart is a missile. Never throw a dart until everyone is behind you.

Just for the information of a new player, the numbering and spacing of the board's sections are always the same, with 20 at the top. The outer ring doubles the score in each section; the inner circle trebles it. In the centre are two small rings which make up the 'bull' or bullseye'; the outer scores 25 and the inner 50.

As you may be playing with some friends who are not very tall, the height at which you hang the board can be a matter of choice. But the strict rule is that the centre of the board should be 1·7 metres from the floor.

Each player has three darts, and the distance at which you stand to throw them should be 2·7 metres. This is called the hockey line, and a player's feet must not be in front of it.

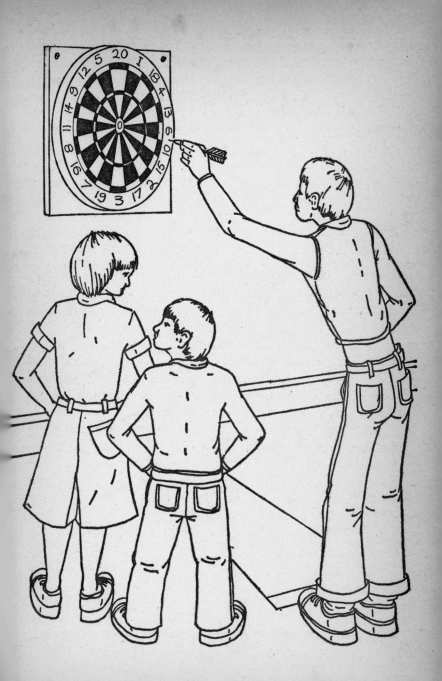

Perhaps you do not have room for this distance, which is a pity, as practice at the correct distance is quite important if you are to continue to play darts when you have grown up, as you almost certainly will.

A game consists of three 'legs', and a leg is the point at which you reach a score one over an even number. A short leg is usually 101, but most players choose 301 as the target.

Mental arithmetic comes in to darts because you do not score up to the total but down from it to zero, so all the time you are deducting your score. Each side has a blackboard or a piece of paper on which the selected score (101 or 301) is written at the top. After each turn the new, lower number is written underneath.

The game starts and ends on a double. A player (or a side when more than two are playing) cannot begin scoring until a double has been obtained. But if, for instance, a player throws his first dart into the outer ring of the segment marked 11, his next two darts can also score.

Perhaps he scores three with the second dart and twenty with the third. The first dart in the double 11 gives him twenty-two. As he is now in play he can add to this figure his scores of three and twenty – a total of forty-five. This he deducts from the marked up target score of 301, crosses out 301 and writes below it 256. Could you have managed those sums in your head?

Darts are thrown in three's until the end of the game approaches. Then there have to be some careful calculations, for the last dart to be thrown must hit a double which will reduce the score to exactly 0.

Suppose at this point you have reduced your total to thirty. One dart in the double ring of the 15 segment will end your game. But the first dart may well go into the single part of the 15 segment. Now you have an odd number, fifteen, for the next two darts.

You will need to aim for a low odd number segment – 1,

3, 5, 7, 9, 11, or 13 – so that you are left with an even number for the third dart. If, for instance, you score in the 9 segment, you now have six (twice three) to get in a double.

You may fail to reduce the score to 2 on this turn (1 is no good as there is no double half for the finish of the game), so you will still have the chance of another attempt at a double on your next turn. But if you go below zero you are said to have 'gone bust'. The score from your turn is ignored and you (or your partner on your side) return to the original score next time round. This is the general rule, though some players consider 'going bust' means you have lost the game.

There are some simpler darts games as regards scoring, but they are rather more difficult to play successfully. **Round the Clock** is a quick game for any number of players. The aim is to throw a dart in sequence into every number from 1 to 20, with three attempts on each turn. Doubles and trebles can be counted when they come in the correct sequence. Thus you can progress from 1 to 2 by throwing into the 2 segment or into the double 1, and from 11 to 12 by getting a 12, a double 6 or a treble 4.

Darts cricket is a game for two players. The winner of a toss decides whether to bat or bowl. The batsman gets runs only when, with his three darts, he scores more than forty. Thus if he gets a 12, a double 6 and a 19 his total is forty-three. He subtracts forty from his total and writes down that he has scored three runs.

The bowler concentrates entirely on the bull. Every dart in the centre ring counts five wickets, every dart in the outer ring of the bull one wicket. When he has taken eleven wickets the players change sides.

Darts Fives is an easy game for any number of players. You do not need a double to start and finish, and the scoring is from zero up to an agreed total – say 100. Each player throws three darts on each turn, and he can only score when the total is divisible by five, the result being his score. **If,** for instance, he obtains one, nine, and four (a total of fourteen), he scores nothing. If he scores one, nine and five (a total of fifteen), he scores three (three fives).

Very accurate darts throwers may like to try their skill at **Shanghai Darts.** In this game the player has to throw his three darts in turn into the same segment, starting at 1 and finishing at 9. It is far more difficult than it sounds, and to prevent the game going on interminably there is usually a rule that any player failing to get three darts on his first attempt into 5 has lost and drops out of the game. In Shanghai Darts the double and treble rings are ignored – thus a dart in either ring in the 3 segment is regarded as a single three.

Table Football

For this game you need a smooth, oblong table, but not a highly polished one, for you may scratch the surface a little during play. If there is a desk in your house, or a table covered with laminated plastic, that would be perfect, and there will be no complaints about damage.

At each end mark the goal posts with a piece of chalk. The distance between them representing the goal should be ten centimetres. Indicate the centre of the table with a small chalk mark.

The ball is a small coin such as a 1p piece or any coin about two centimetres in circumference. At the start of the game it is at the centre of the pitch. The players are coins up to twice the size of the ball. A 2p piece is ideal. If there are two people to play the game then just two coins to represent the players will be sufficient. With two or more on each side you can have up to three coins per team. To identify them, one side plays with heads showing, the other with tails. To start the game, line up your players by the ball, each team defending its goal.

You play by holding a coin (a 2p piece for instance) between thumb and forefinger and knocking any one of your own players to hit the ball or to get into a better position – perhaps to block an opposing player or to be ready for a goal kick on the next turn.

If there is a hit of any kind, it must first be on the ball. Hitting an opposing player before hitting the ball is a foul and gives the opponent a double turn.

If the ball is knocked off the table, either on the sides or at the ends on either side of the goal, the opposing player takes a kick from the spot where the ball left the table, moving any one of his own coins and any one of his opponent's he wishes to place his own coin on the edge of the table, the 'ball' touching it, and the opposing player touching the 'ball', the three coins making a straight line at right angles to the edge of the table.

After a goal is scored play is resumed from the centre. To avoid disputes about goals it is a good idea for one player to hold his fingers as goal posts on the chalk spots before a goal kick is taken.

Practice will show that shots to position the 'ball' and to obstruct the opponent make this a fascinating and skilful game. Players soon learn that vigorous shots which simply knock coins off the table are not the way to win.

Dominoes

If you play dominoes regularly you will certainly not regard it as just a 'kids' game'. No one knows how old it is, though the Chinese are believed to have invented marked pieces of ivory or bone thousands of years ago. Travelling merchants from Venice brought specimens of Chinese dominoes with them. It was in Italy in the Middle Ages that the present black and white pattern was devised, with the name taken from the dominoes, or masks, worn by guests at dances and parties. A domino set consists of twenty-eight pieces, each marked with a pair of numbers in any combination from zero to six.

To be regarded as a dominoes expert you should use the many unusual names and terms of the game. A domino piece is a bone (which, of course, is what they were originally made from). The unplayed dominoes are said to be in the boneyard. A double (a piece carrying two identical numbers), when placed crosswise, is called a chevvy (from the French *à cheval*, meaning on horseback). A bone of a greater value than an opponent's is heavier (not higher) than his lighter (not lower) one. You don't say 'can't go' when you miss a turn, but knock on the table with an unplayed domino.

Now for some domino games. Most of them can be played by two to six people, always leaving some bones in the boneyard after all the players have drawn their hand. In the simpler games two players each draw thirteen of the bones which are lying face down, leaving two in the boneyard. Three players draw eight each, leaving four. Four players draw six each, leaving four. Five players draw five each, leaving three. Six players draw four each, leaving four. When there are different rules, you will read about the number of bones to be drawn.

The game is usually started by the player with the heaviest bone – double 6 or double 5. If two players hold a bone of the same weight, say a double 5 and a 6–4, the double takes priority. He puts this bone face up on the table and the game proceeds. When his turn arrives, each player selects a bone which carries on one end a number matching either end of the layout on the table. He adds it to the layout, with matching numbers touching.

Running Out is the simplest game. It is just a matter of matching numbers, placing a 3 against a 3, a blank against a blank, and so on. Doubles are always placed crosswise, the next bone being matched to one half of the double. Thus a double 3 must have a 3 placed against it, not a 6. When there is a choice as to which end to cover, the player should consider which choice would be most likely to prevent his opponent playing one of his bones.

If a player cannot go he misses his turn, coming into the game next time round. If no player can proceed then the player who first failed to go draws one bone from the boneyard, and if he still cannot go the next player draws one, and so on until someone can go or the boneyard is empty.

The winner is the first to play all his bones. If the game comes to a stop before this, the player with the lowest number of pips on his unplayed bones is the winner.

Each player counts up the pips on his unplayed bones and the total is kept on a piece of paper. The game stops when one player passes fifty or one hundred (depending on how long you want to play), and the player with the lowest total is the winner.

In **Blocking,** a game for two players, the object is to get rid of all your heavy bones and prevent your opponent doing so. Bones are played as in Running Out, one side of a domino matched to the next and a double placed crosswise.

When one player cannot go the pips of his unplayed bones are counted and his opponent adds this number to the total of pips on his own unplayed bones. The highest score attained after, say, half an hour's play, indicates the winner.

This sounds a simple game, but it needs a lot of careful play. You have to decide between the need to get rid of heavy bones so that they are not left in your hand if your opponent prevents you going on your turn, and the need to hold on to bones with a high total of pips if you feel confident of winning.

In **All Threes** each player draws five bones, which means that from two to five people can play, in the last case only three being left in the boneyard.

The object is to play your bone so that when it is in position the pips at each end of the layout add up to three or a multiple of three, and you add this total to your score. But the newly played bone must match as in simple running out games. Therefore you will not always score.

The player who draws double 6 starts the game. This bone's pips total twelve, which is his score, written down on a piece of paper. If the next player has the 6–3 he is luckier still, for he places it against the double 6, laid crosswise to the row soon to be made, and he has twelve at one end and three at the other, a score of fifteen. But if his bone with a 6 on it is the 6–5, 6–4, 6–2, or 6–1, he will not score anything, as the ends would then add up to a total which is not a multiple of three. The 6–0, however, would give him a score of twelve.

A player who has no bones with pips enabling him to play must draw from the boneyard until he can. When the boneyard is exhausted he passes, and the next player continues the round.

When the game ends because one player has used all his bones or no one can continue, some rather tricky scoring takes place. This can greatly change the outcome.

There are two things which can happen. First, if the game stops because no one can continue but everyone still has unplayed bones, the winner is the player with the lowest number of pips on unplayed bones. He gets bonus marks of three for this. But he may still be the real loser because other players have scored more than him during the game.

In the second ending, where the game is won by the player disposing of all his bones, there is a big bonus for him. He adds to his score a number based on the total of pips on the unplayed bones of all the opponents divided by three. Thus, let us say that there are two losing players. One has bones with pips totalling seventeen, and the other pips totalling twenty-four. That makes a total of forty-one. The nearest multiple of three to forty-one is three times fourteen (making forty-two), and so fourteen is the figure added to the winner's score.

If the total had been forty the nearest multiple would have been three times thirteen (giving thirty-nine) and the bonus would then have been thirteen.

There are many other domino games played in different countries, but we will describe one that is known all over the world, and is probably the best of any. It is called **Matador**, and is best when played by two people.

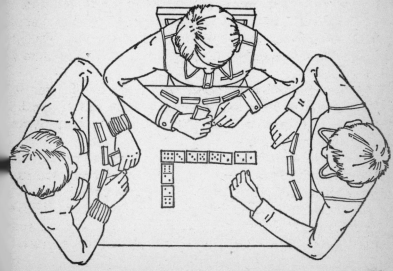

You forget the usual practice of having to match a bone at one end of the layout. Instead the object is to play a bone so that its end pips added to the pips exposed at the other end of the layout total seven.

Doubles are not placed as chevvies (crosswise) but lengthwise. As a result only one end of a double is counted. The player who draws the highest double starts the game (though of course the two ends of a double never total seven).

After the double 6, for example, has been played, the next player can use any bone with one pip at one end, covering one side of the double 6 and using the other to add to the one he has placed at the other end, making a total of seven.

You may be thinking that the game must soon come to an end with the need always to make ends totalling seven, but there are valuable bones called Matadors.

These are the double blank, the 4-3, 5-2, and 6-1. They can be played either way round and the ends of the layout need not make a total of seven. Obviously only a Matador can be played when both ends are blank.

Matadors are so valuable that none should be played until there is no other bone in your hand which can be used. You should never play one just to make a total of seven with both ends of the layout, if you have another suitable bone.

A player who cannot make a total of seven and has no Matador must draw from the boneyard and go on doing so until he can play, but the last two bones are never drawn. When that stage is reached the player misses his turn.

The game ends when one player is out or neither can play. A winner who is out takes as his score the total of pips left on his opponent's unplayed dominoes.

When the game is blocked, the winner is the player with the lower total of pips on unplayed bones, and his score is the figure left after he deducts the number of pips on his unplayed bones from his opponent's.

If you want to play a Matador session like the experts you will go on playing until one player scores 120.

Did you know you can play dominoes without an opponent? This game is called **Domino Patience**. You shuffle the dominoes face downwards, and pick out five. Then play in the usual way, matching number against similar number. When play is no longer possible, you draw pieces to make up the total in your hand to five again, and continue until either you have played all the dominoes, or you cannot play, or there are not enough dominoes in reserve to make up your hand to five.

It sounds as if you can always play right out, but unless you carefully watch your every move you will probably get stuck.

Draughts

You probably know how to play draughts, the game known as Checkers in America. Just to remind you of the simple rules, it is played on a board of 64 black and white squares in eight rows of eight. Each player has twelve draughtsmen, one set being white and one black. These are placed on the black squares of the first three rows of the board at each end, and throughout the game black squares only are used.

A move is one square diagonally forward to a vacant square, but a draught reaching the last row on the far side becomes a King and can then move forwards or backwards. A King is indicated by placing two draughtsmen together, one on top of the other.

The object is to capture opposing draughts by jumping over them to a vacant square, after which the piece jumped over is removed from the board. If, after one capture, the draught can take another opposing piece and perhaps more after that, these moves can be made during a single turn.

A draught which can make a capture but does not do so is 'huffed', which means it is removed from the board.

The loser of the game is the player who finds himself unable to make a move.

The more expert you are at playing draughts, the more difficult you will probably find **Losing Draughts**, in which you must try to lose your own men instead of taking your opponent's.

You set out the men in the usual manner, and the moves are just the same as in normal play. Your opponent's draughts must be taken whenever the situation requires it. Sometimes there will be a choice of capture, when, of course, you must decide which move will benefit you most.

Chase the Treasure

You play this game for two on a draughts board with six draughts for each player, one having black pieces and the other white.

At the start each player arranges his draughts on his end of the board as follows: four in the centre square of the back row and two in the centre of the row above them. Thus there are two spaces on each side in the rear row and three spaces on each side in the row above it.

By tossing a coin decide which side starts with possession of the treasure, which can be a small coin, a counter, or anything which will rest safely on one of the draughts. The winner of the toss can select whichever draught he prefers to carry the treasure.

Each side, with or without the treasure at the start, has to try to carry it across the board to the other side. Players take turns to move their draughts one square at a time forwards, backwards or sideways, but not diagonally. Both colour squares are used. In order to capture the treasure a player must get one of his draughts into a square next to the draught carrying it, and with a vacant square on the other side. He does not jump over the treasure draught (there is no jumping in this game) but transfers the treasure on to the capturing draught, the game then resuming. Unlike ordinary draughts, players do not capture and remove each other's pieces in this game.

The first player to carry the treasure to the opposite base line is the winner.

This is quite a difficult game to play. While the side without the treasure has to concentrate on getting beside the draught with the treasure, the other side's main object is to protect it by surrounding it with his other pieces. Then, when possession changes sides, the tactics of each player have to be reversed.

Reversing

In this game for two players you need a draughts board and two sets of thirty-two coins or counters with a contrasting colour on the underside. As it is a problem to collect sixty-four coins, and not many two-tone counters are sold, the simplest thing may be to cut your counters out from a sheet of cardboard which is white on one side and straw-coloured on the other. Failing this, you can colour a sheet of cardboard on one side and then cut it up into sixty-four small pieces.

To explain the game we will assume that one player has white pieces and the other black (the undersides will, of course, be in the opponent's colour).

The first player puts one of his pieces on one of the four centre squares of the board, his opponent puts a piece in one of the three remaining squares, and during the next two turns the other remaining squares of the four in the centre are filled.

The next turn must follow the two basic rules of the game – first, the piece the player adds to the board must be in line, across, down or diagonally, with one of the pieces he has already played, and second it must be next to one of his opponent's pieces. These rules apply right through the game.

But here is the danger. Any piece caught between an opponent's two pieces is turned over or reversed, and thus goes over to the opponent's side.

Quite soon a player will find that he cannot comply with the rules about his piece being in line with one of his own pieces and next to an opponent's piece. He then has to miss a turn.

Eventually so many pieces belonging to one player have been reversed and thus gone over to the opponent's side that the first player cannot play any longer, and his opponent has won.

Security Draughts

On a draughts board start with the spy (a black draught) in one of the end squares of the base line.

The fortress is marked with a square piece of paper or cardboard in the corner of the other base line which lies

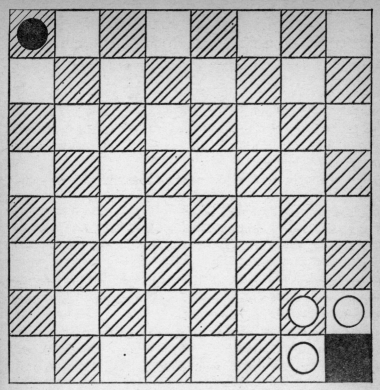

diagonally opposite. The security guards of the fortress are three white draughts, and at the start of the game they are placed in the three squares adjoining the corner square on which the fortress stands (see the sketch). One player is the spy and the other security. No other pieces are used.

The spy moves towards the fortress and the security draughtsmen move out to capture him. The spy can kill – remove – a security man if he can jump him from an adjacent square to a vacant one on the other side, and the security men can do the same with the spy. The spy's object is, of course, to land on the fortress square.

There is one big difference from ordinary draughts. Moves and 'kills' are made one square at a time, backwards, forwards, sideways, but not diagonally.

Squails

Drake and his friends doubtless played this game in their Devon homes when the weather was too bad for playing bowls in the open air. It remained a popular game for young and old until shove ha'penny, which is rather similar, ousted it.

The attraction of squails is that you do not have to have a special board. Any smooth table, preferably a round or oval one, will do.

The squails were originally metal discs two centimetres in diameter, and each player had three or four. A small coin was placed in the middle of the table, and the player's object was to shoot a squail from the edge of the table, aiming at the coin in the centre and using the palm of the hand, the winner being the player who had one squail closest to the centre coin.

You can play the game with a small coin in the centre, say a British 1p, and each player having three coins about twice as large, say 2p pieces. Each player shoots his coin in turn, and he can of course knock any squail, either his own or an opponent's, out of position, or hit the target coin. But if he knocks the target coin off the table he is out of the game.

The winner is the player with a squail nearest to the target coin when all squails have been played. In the old days there were big arguments about the closest squail and players had a special measuring stick called a swoggle. You can use a ruler marked in centimetres to settle a claim.

Card Games

Card Dropping

This game is good fun at parties if you can make up two teams of at least five players in each.

Place two kitchen chairs, or chairs with fairly high backs, at one end of the room, a little distance apart and with their backs nearest the end of the room. Place two basins or cardboard boxes, not more than fifteen centimetres wide, behind the chairs and about thirty centimetres from the chairs' back legs.

Deal out the cards so that everyone in both teams has the same number. Thus with a total of ten players you can give each team member five each.

On the word go the first member of each team holding his cards goes to the chair, kneels with one leg on the seat, and keeps the foot of his other leg on the ground. He rests one arm on the top of the chair back and then passes the cards up one at a time from the other hand to the extended arm and tries to drop them into the basin or box.

The arm resting on the chair back must not be lifted out of contact with the chair back and the foot touching the floor must not be raised. You will probably need an umpire to see these rules are not disobeyed.

It sounds simple, but it will be surprising how many cards flutter outside their target.

The team with the most cards successfully dropped is the winner.

Snap

Almost everyone knows this game for two or more players, but just as a reminder, here's how it should be played. A whole pack of cards is dealt out and the players hold their cards face downwards without looking at them. Each in turn then takes his top card and, turning it away from him, quickly places it face upwards in the centre of the table.

As soon as a card appears which is of the same value as the preceding one, 'Snap!' should be called out, the first player to do so picking up all the cards and adding them to his hand. Eventually one player has collected all the cards and is the winner.

Snap can be rather noisy, but you can play a silent version with no calling out, when whoever has played the card matching the previous one takes the whole pile. The silent game is liable to go on for rather a long time.

Donkey

A card game to play as quietly as possible, for the whole point is to avoid being the loser through failing to notice what the other players (any number from four to thirteen) are doing.

Prepare a pack of cards by selecting sets of four cards of each value according to the number of players. Thus for five players you could select sets of four of Kings, Queens, Jacks, tens and nines. But the actual value of the sets does not matter.

Shuffle them thoroughly and then deal four face down to each player.

After looking at them, each player, starting with the one

to the left of the dealer, passes an unwanted card to the player on his left, in the hope of getting four cards of the same value.

When a player has completed his set he should, as quietly and secretively as he can, place his cards face upwards on the table. He can do this at any time after his turn has given him the set but before his next turn.

The other players must immediately lay down their cards. The last to do so is Donkey.

Patience

There are many hundreds of Patience games, all designed for a solitary player, though there is no reason why two should not participate as allies rather than opponents. But one player should be the actual mover of the cards and the other the adviser, or fierce arguments are likely!

A few games depend on nothing but luck; most require skill and careful forethought before a move is made, but even in the most difficult Patience games luck plays a big part.

Here are four games to pass a half hour or so, and to introduce you to a recreation which will intrigue you all your life.

All Fours is a simple Patience game. The object is to arrange all cards of the same face value in order from Ace (1) to Kings. You do not bother about the suits.

After shuffling the pack, deal the cards face downwards in three rows – five stacks in the top row, five in the second, and three in the bottom row. Thus there will be four cards in each stack.

In your mind's eye regard these stacks as the order of the

cards in sequence: Ace–5 in the top row; 6–10 in the second; Jack, Queen, King in the bottom row.

To start your game turn up the top left-hand card, check its value, and place it face upwards almost under the stack where it should belong to make the sequence. Thus, if you turn up a 9, you push it under the four cards in the fourth stack of the second row, leaving enough showing to identify it.

Now you turn up the top card in the stack to which you have just added a card (in the example, the top card above the exposed 9).

Continue picking up cards in this way and placing them in their correct sequence until all the cards have been turned up and are in numerical order.

You may think that you will always complete the game. In fact you will find that frequently you reach a situation where, having placed three Aces in the right position, you then find the fourth. Then there is no additional card to turn up in that stack. You are, in the language of Patience, chockered.

If you wish, you can give yourself one more chance. When chockered after finding all four Aces, for example, you can continue by drawing a card from the stack to the left of the one from which you drew that fourth Ace, or if that was at the left hand end of a row, from the right hand stack of the row above it. This may enable you to complete the game, though it is by no means a certainty.

The Pyramid is based on pairing cards so that the pips of the two cards add up to thirteen. An Ace counts as one, a Jack as eleven and a Queen twelve. Kings are not used for pairing but will be laid aside during play.

Make a pyramid shape with twenty-eight cards in seven rows – all the cards face downwards except those in the bottom row.

Start at the top with one card. Below it, lay two cards

just overlapping the bottom corners of the top card. Three cards next, then four, five, six, and finally seven in the bottom row – these seven cards, remember, are laid face upwards. All the rows just overlap the cards above them as explained for the second row.

Place the undealt cards – twenty-four of them – in a stack, face upwards, to one side of your pyramid. This is called the discard pile.

All seven cards in the bottom row are available to start play. Remove any two cards which add up to thirteen. They can be two from the bottom row, or one from that row together with the top card of the discard pile. In the latter case a new card is exposed on the discard pile and gives another chance to make a pair totalling thirteen.

As soon as two neighbouring cards are removed by pairing, the card above the space is free to be turned face upwards and can be used for another pairing. So you should always favour pairing adjacent cards so that the card above them may be turned up. As Kings are not used for pairing they can be removed whenever they appear.

As the game is often liable to get chockered with no pairing possible, you can relax the rules a little by allowing three turns of the cards on the discard pile, placing the cards from it which you reject at the bottom of the pile.

For the very simple game of **One-and-Six** you need two packs of cards. Deal a row of four cards, face upwards, then lay two cards aside in what is called the rubbish heap. Repeat the deal of four cards to the row and two to the heap until the pack is used up.

But do this slowly because every time you find an Ace or a King you lay them aside. As soon as any of these cards have been discovered – but only one of each suit even though two of each kind exists in the packs – you can start adding to them as you deal whenever a card of the same suit and the next value appears.

For example, you find the Ace of Clubs. Next you need to watch for the 2 of Clubs. Then you find the King of Hearts, so you hope to get the Queen of Hearts, so it is up from the Ace and down from the King of each suit.

When you have dealt all the cards pick up the rubbish heap, without shuffling it, and deal four cards on to the row, removing those which will correctly fit on your Ace and King batches. You can do this three times to complete the eight built-up suits in sequence, up or down. If cards are still unplaced you have been chockered and need to start a new game.

The Clock does not always work out, but when it does it is interesting to time yourself and see how quickly you can manage to complete it.

Incidentally, in the United States the Clock is known as Solitaire, but in the Old World Solitaire is a game played with marbles on a specially designed board.

Make the pattern of a clock face by laying a pack of cards face downwards in a circle of twelve positions and one position in the centre.

Start dealing at the centre, then in the one o'clock position, round to twelve, and so on, so that there will be four cards in each of the thirteen positions.

Turn up the top card in the centre stack and place it, face upwards, just under the stack it ought to go – the 7 of Hearts at seven o'clock, the Jack of Spades at eleven o'clock, and so on. The Kings go in the centre.

The moves after the first one are made by turning up the top card on the stack under which a card has been placed at the previous move, and so on until all cards are face upwards in their correct positions.

Sevens

Each player is dealt seven cards (two, three, or four can play). The rest of the pack is placed in a pile face downwards on the table. The first player puts a card face upwards on the table. It must be followed by a card of the same value or the same suit. Thus if the first card is the 4 of Hearts, any 4 or any Heart may be played by the next player.

Anyone who cannot play a suitable card must draw from the pack until he has a playable card.

The winner is the player who first gets rid of all his cards or, when all the cards in the pack have been drawn, the player who holds the lowest number of cards.

Cheating

Two packs of playing cards are needed for this game, and any number over two can play. Deal out all the cards, and don't worry if some players have more cards than the others. It will not affect the result.

The player to the left of the dealer plays one of his cards face downwards into the centre of the table. It can be any card he likes but he will be wise to get rid of a low one. As he puts the card down he calls out what he claims to be its value, with Ace counting as 1, and the court cards named.

The next player then plays a card which he claims is one value higher than the previous one. Thus if the first player has called 3 the next one calls 4. If the latter player is wise and has a 4 he should play it (honesty, as in all activities, is the best policy)! But if he has no 4, he must put down any card, calling 4. The game continues in this way, with the next player calling 5, the next 6, and so on.

At any point in the game any player can call 'cheat!' when another names his card. The latter must then turn up the card he is playing. If the card is not of the value named, then the cheater must pick up all the cards laid down in the centre. But if he had not been cheating, then the challenger must pick up all the cards.

Each time there is a challenge the winner of that challenge starts a new round of play, and a new round is started by the neighbour of the player who calls King (the highest card).

The player who first gets rid of all his cards is the winner.

Old Maid

It's called a kids' game, and it is. But it is so old that you will find that all your aged relations will like to play it because they did so way back in the dim and distant past. Anyway, it is good fun, and for as many players as you like.

From a pack of cards remove one Queen. (If more than six people are playing it makes a better game to use two packs, but still removing a Queen from only one pack.)

Deal out the cards, and don't worry if the number of cards is not the same for each player.

The players pick up their cards and place all the pairs (i.e. two cards of the same number) in their hand face downwards on the table. This should reduce the number of cards to be held to a fairly reasonable handful even for very young players.

Fanning out his handful of cards a little, the player to the left of the dealer offers them, face downwards, to his neighbour, who takes any card he likes from the handful. If the card he has taken makes a pair he discards this and then offers his fanned out cards to *his* neighbour, and so on round and round the table.

Eventually all the possible pairs will have been discarded and one player is left with one Queen, and is Old Maid.

You can consider him/her the winner or loser just as you prefer. We prefer the former. Who wouldn't be proud to own a Queen?

Rummy

Almost everyone who enjoys card-playing has his own
version of Rummy, and it is wise to talk about the rules of
your particular game before you start, or there may be
arguments. If you really wanted to learn the original version
you would have to go to Mexico, where it originated as
Con Quien, Spanish for 'with whom'.

First we will explain the simplest of all Rummy games. It
is for two, three or four players. If more than four are
playing two packs should be used.

Deal seven cards to each player. The remainder are placed
face downwards in the centre of the table and are known as
the stock, and the top card is turned face upwards alongside
the stock to form the discard pile. A pencil and paper are
needed for keeping the score.

The object of the game is to collect three or more cards
of the same suit in sequence (with the Ace counted either as
1 or above the King) and/or sets of three or four cards of the
same value. Thus a sequence might be 4, 5 and 6 of Clubs,
and a set might consist of three or four Queens.

After checking the seven cards he has been dealt at
the begininng of the game each player, beginning with the
player on the left of the dealer, must either pick up the
exposed card or try his luck with the top (unexposed)
card on the stock. He exchanges the card he has taken for
one in his hand, and puts the latter face upwards on the
discard pile.

If after this exchange all of a player's seven cards are in
sets or sequences he lays them down face upwards. There is
then no score against him. He can also lay down his cards
when he has six of them in sets or sequences, so long as the
unmatched card is not higher than a 6. The score against
him is then the value of the odd card.

As soon as any player lays down his cards all the other

players must do the same. The score against them is the total of pips on the cards which they have not matched in sequences or sets. Court cards carry a penalty score of eleven each, and Aces fifteen each.

To make the game more exciting the Joker can be left in the pack and can represent any value, though a player may not use it in one of his sets or sequences to represent a card which he had put in his other set or sequence. Thus, the Joker could count as 4 of Clubs in a set of four, along with the 4 of Hearts, Spades and Diamonds, but it could not be used in this way if the player also tried to present a sequence of 3 of Clubs, 4 of Clubs and 5 of Clubs.

Another idea for increasing the luck of the game is to count all 2s as 'wild', which means that they can represent any value in their suit.

The game ends when one player has a total of 100 penalty points, the winner being the player with the lowest score.

When you are familiar with the simple game you may like to play more complicated versions of Rummy.

In one popular game, **Display Rummy,** the number of cards dealt out varies according to the number of players. With two players each is dealt ten cards, with three players seven and with four or more players six.

The undealt cards are placed face downwards in the centre of the table, with the top card turned face upwards alongside them, as in the basic game. Players have the choice of the exposed card or the top card on the stock.

The difference in this game is that any set or sequence is placed face upwards in front of the player as he completes it, after which he must of course remember to add a card to the discard pile.

As each player's turn comes round he may, if he wishes, get rid of any cards which fit on to an opponent's exposed set or sequence. For example, if one player lays down three Jacks any of his opponents can add the Jack he holds when his turn comes. If there is an exposed sequence of, say, 6, 7 and 8 of Clubs, he can add the 5 of Clubs at one end and/or the 9 of Clubs at the other.

When one player gets rid of all his cards either by making sets and sequences of his own or by fitting them on to his opponents' displayed sets and sequences and putting his last card on the discard pile, the game ends.

In this version of Rummy there is no penalty score, but instead the winner receives a score made up of the total of all the pips on his opponents' unmatched cards, with Court cards counting eleven and Aces fifteen. Play of the game ends when one player has scored 200 or more.

Risky Rummy is well named, for courage brings great rewards but undue risks carry heavy penalties.

Seven cards are dealt to each player, with the usual stock and discard piles in the centre of the table.

Play continues as usual, with a choice of the exposed or unexposed card, but the discarded card is placed so that it only partly overlaps the card below it, enabling the values of all the exposed cards to be seen.

Sets and sequences are placed face upwards in front of the player as he makes them. An opponent can complete or add to these displayed sets, but puts the cards involved down in front of himself, at the same time stating what he is doing. Thus, with three 7s laid down by one player, an opponent lays down his 7 in front of himself, at the same time saying 'My 7 to complete John's set of 7s.'

Now for another big difference. When a player's turn comes round he may need one of the underneath cards from the discard pile. He can take this card and use it in his display during that turn, but must also take all the cards above it.

A player may therefore feel justified, after obtaining two Jacks during play, to pick up several cards in order to obtain a third Jack. He must decide whether this is worth the risk, as it means he also has to take several cards lying above the Jack.

Fortunately you can get a good idea of the risks involved because each player's score is kept as the game proceeds. One player should keep the totals, calling out each person's score after his turn.

Cards laid down in sets or sequences, or laid down as part of them in front of an opponent, score according to their value. Court cards count eleven each. Aces in sets count fifteen each, but only one point in a sequence of Ace, 2 and 3.

It will be seen that big scores are possible – forty-five for three Aces, thirty-three for Jack, Queen, King, for instance.

The player who gets rid of all his cards and calls out 'Rummy risked' adds to his score the value of the cards left in his opponents' hands (with any unmatched Ace counting fifteen). A greedy player who has, on the previous turn, picked up a handful of cards just to get hold of a required matching card, may therefore be left with an assortment which puts him far down the list of scores as he adds a large number to the winner's score.

The usual end of the game comes when one player scores 500.

Finally, why not try the game which is often mentioned in American films and TV shows – **Gin Rummy ?**

The name has nothing to do with an animal trap or drink, but is the English speaking version of *Con Quien*, the Spanish–Mexican name we mentioned earlier, the 'Quien' becoming 'Gin'.

Gin Rummy is a game for two players. They cut for deal, the lowest card winning (Ace equals one).

The dealer distributes the cards – eleven to his opponent and ten to himself. The rest of the pack is placed face downwards in the centre of the table.

Play starts with the opponent discarding one card face upwards alongside the unexposed stack, to form the beginning of a discard pile. Players now have ten cards. The

dealer can take this card or try his luck with the top card on the stock and play continues in this way.

When one player has matched all his cards into sequences of three or more, or sets of three or four, and also got rid of his remaining card to the discard pile, he calls 'Gin'. He gets thirty points for winning, plus the total of pips on the unmatched cards in his opponent's hand. Aces count one point, Court cards ten each.

It is not essential to get rid of all cards to win. A player may knock on the table and expose his hand (without calling 'Gin'), when his unmatched cards total ten points or under.

He is, of course, hoping that his opponent has unmatched cards with more pips than his ten. It may well not be so, for the opponent has one last chance to stave off serious defeat. He can add any cards to the knocking player's sequence or set. If, for instance, a player knocks and lays down 2, 3 and 4 of Diamonds, and a set of three 9s, and his opponent has an unmatched Ace or 5 of Diamonds and/or the remaining 9, he can lay them down, thus reducing greatly his number of unmatched cards.

When the game ends by knocking, the knocking player gets no bonus as he would with a call of 'Gin', but earns points to the value of his opponent's unmatched cards after his own total of unmatched value is deducted. For example, he may knock with a surplus of six. The opponent has to admit that he has been left with a King and a 7, valued at seventeen. The player who knocked then gets a score of eleven.

There are times when the knocking player finds his opponent's unmatched cards yield a total of pips the same as, or lower than, his own. In that case the opponent wins a bonus of ten points taken from the knocking player's total, plus any difference in the number of pips. It is therefore quite possible for the player who knocks because he is confident of being the winner, to find himself the loser.

If you ever play Gin Rummy with Americans who say they prefer 'the old-fashioned Gin', it will probably mean that they play a game with two additional rules.

The first is that the suit of the first card exposed in the discard pile is important: if it is a Spade, the score made at the end of the game (excluding the bonus) is doubled.

The second rule is that this starting card also controls the maximum figure on which a player may knock. If, therefore, the turned-up card is the 2 of Spades, knocking can occur only when the player's spare card is an Ace or a 2 (or, in a rare instance, two Aces), and the points earned are doubled.

Gin Rummy games should continue until one player scores 100 and is the winner.

Chase the Ace

A very simple game, where luck counts for much more than skill, and any number from four upwards can play.

You need a pack of cards and enough counters to give three to each player.

The dealer hands out one card to each player, face downwards. Each player looks at his card and hopes that it is not the lowest. Ace counts as one, and in the suits Clubs are lowest, followed by Diamonds, then Hearts, and Spades are the highest. Thus the Ace of Diamonds is lower than the Ace of Spades.

Anyone holding a King places it face upwards on the table. The others, beginning with the player on the left of the dealer, can change their chosen card with the player to the left if they wish, or they may decide to keep their own. They cannot swap cards if the neighbour has laid down a King. His neighbour must stick to the card he holds.

The dealer is luckier. The player on his right cannot demand the dealer's card, and the dealer can either stick with the card he has, or if it is a low one, he can exchange it, without looking, for any card in the undealt pack.

Now all the players place their cards, face upwards, on the table. The player with the lowest card has to pay one counter to the winner in order to remain in the game.

The dealer repeats the deal of one card to each player and the game proceeds as before.

The player with the lowest card must pay a counter every time, and so he has only three chances to stay in the game unless he has won some counters in a previous round. Eventually only one player will be left and he is the winner, taking all the counters used in the game. This will give him a head start for the next game!

Cribbage

If you enjoy card games, but have not so far learned how to play cribbage, you have missed what is surely the best card game for two players. It is a fairly complicated game as regards scoring, but quite easy to play.

Cribbage is won by the first player to score sixty-one points. These are usually marked on a special board with four rows of thirty holes, two on each side, and two game holes at one end of the board. Starting at the game holes end of the board, each player marks his score by moving pegs along a corresponding number of holes, working his way down the outer edge of the board and then back up the inner row.

The values of the cards are Ace (1) to 10, the Court cards each counting ten. Points are scored by cards totalling fifteen, sequences, pairs, by making a total of thirty-one, or getting nearest to that total (known as 'one for go').

Players take turns to deal. To begin playing the dealer gives five cards to his opponent and himself, then cutting the rest of the pack and turning up the top card (called the Start). If this Start card is a Jack the dealer get two points ('two for his heels').

Each player then disposes of two of his five cards, face downwards, to form the Crib, which belongs to the dealer. To compensate for this advantage the non-dealer scores three points.

The non-dealer starts play, putting down one of his three cards face upwards in front of him, at the same time calling out the value. The dealer then plays a card, calling out the total made by his card and the previous one. This continues towards a total of thirty-one, which must not be exceeded under any circumstances. A player who cannot play a card which will keep the total below thirty-one misses a turn, calling 'go'.

Scoring takes place during play as follows:

Two points for the player who makes a total of fifteen (e.g. 9 of Hearts followed by 2 of Spades followed by 4 of Diamonds).

Two points for pairs (a card of the same value as the card just played). Court cards must be of equal rank, i.e. a King with a King.

Six points for royal pairs – a third card of the same value as the two cards which have previously made a pair.

Twelve points for double royal pairs – a fourth card of the same value as the previous three.

One point for each card in a run of three or more cards. Run cards need not have been played in sequence, 6–4–5 counting three points just as well as 4–5–6.

One point for last play (the card which brings the total nearest to thirty-one), and two points for making exactly thirty-one.

When thirty-one is reached, players move into the second stage of the game – the Show. Each player picks up the cards which have been played and placed in front of him, and adds their score to his total. The non-dealer scores first. He combines the values of his three cards with the value of the Start card, so he has four cards with which to gain points. These are the scores:

'One for a Knave'. A Jack in the hand of the same suit as the start card scores one point.

Fifteens. Every combination of cards in the hand with the Start card totalling fifteen scores two points.

Pairs, Royal Pairs and Double Royal Pairs. Scores of two, six and twelve points as during play, with the Start card used in the pairing.

Runs. Three points for each run of three cards, plus an extra point for each additional card in sequence. Alternative runs each count separately. Thus a player with two 5s and a 7, with the Start card a 6, has two runs of three cards, the two 5s each making a separate run with the 6 and 7.

Flush. One point for each card totalling three or more in sequence and of the same suit; this score in addition to that for a Run.

The dealer works out his score in the same way, and adds to it by exposing the Crib – the two cards from each player disposed of at the start of play. He uses the Start card in calculating his score, so he has five cards with which to make up combinations as explained above. The exception is that for a Flush from the Crib he must present all five cards of the same suit, for which he scores five. He also has the chance of a bonus of one point if the Crib contains a Jack of the same suit as the Start card.

The first player to score sixty-one or over wins the game.

Go Fishing

If you are not too familiar with cards this is an easy game. It can be played by two to four players.

Deal out seven cards each if there are two or three players, five if four are playing. Place the undealt cards face downwards in the centre of the table.

Each player, after deciding which set of four he wants to collect, asks his neighbour on his left, 'Have you any . . .?' naming the cards he wants. Thus, if he is hoping to collect four Queens, he says, 'Have you any Queens?'

If the questioned player has any of the named cards he must hand them over. If he hasn't, he says, 'Go fishing'. The questioner then picks up the top card on the pack in the centre of the table. If he is lucky he shows it to the other players, to prove it is of the value he was demanding.

He can now repeat his demand, though of course for a different value, with an eye to collecting another set of four. If he is exceptionally lucky and, after being told to go fishing, he again picks up the named card from the pack, he again has another turn. Otherwise the questioned player now has his turn with the partner on his left, and so on round the players.

As soon as a player has a set of four he must lay it down, face upwards, on the table. He gets an extra turn for doing so.

Sometimes a lucky and clever player will become the winner by getting rid of all of his cards either by passing them on or by picking up the required card for a set of four from his neighbour and the pack. But often the game comes to a stop because the pack of cards in the centre is exhausted. In that case the player with the largest number of sets is the winner.

Newmarket

Suggest this game to the grown-ups around your home and you will find some eager players, for it is popular with adults even though it is very simple.

You really need two packs of cards because you have to use the Ace of Spades, the King of Diamonds, the Queen of Hearts and the Jack of Clubs separately. However, if you do not have a spare pack, small pieces of paper cut roughly to the size of a card, marked with the above values, will be quite all right. Arrange them in a row at one side of the table.

There should be at least four players, and each should be given ten or more counters for investment.

Each player stakes a counter or counters on one or more of the cards (or paper versions).

Next the other cards are dealt out, with one hand more than the number of players. This extra hand is put aside and never used or examined during play.

The player to the left of the dealer starts, playing any suit he likes, but with the lowest card he holds in that suit. He lays it face up well below the target card of that suit. If, for instance, he plays the 3 of Hearts, he places it in an imaginary column below the target Queen of Hearts. As he places the card he calls out the value and suit just to help the other players.

Whoever has the 4 of Hearts (and it may well be the original player) lays it above the 3 of Hearts and calls out the value. The game continues in this way until the sequence of increasing numbers comes to an end, either because the required card is obviously in the hand of cards put aside, or because the target card has been reached, in which case the counters on it are taken by the person who laid down the last card.

The player who laid down the last card in a sequence then

starts another sequence, again playing any card he wishes as long as it is the lowest of that suit in his hand.

A player who gets rid of all his cards brings the game to a stop, even though one or more of the target cards have not been reached. The counters on them remain to be won in a subsequent game, when all cards except the targets are collected, shuffled and dealt again, the players again staking counters.

The player who first gets rid of his cards obtains an extra reward. He collects one counter for every card left in his opponents' hands.

Pip

This is a card game for parties, for it really needs from six to ten players to make it an exciting battle of wits.

Two packs of cards are shuffled together, and then cut to decide the trump suit. (A trump suit is especially privileged to win over cards of other suits.) Seven cards are dealt to each player. The undealt part of the double pack is placed face downwards in the centre of the table.

Scoring is rather involved so someone has to jot down the totals under each player's name both during and after a game. The object is to win tricks (i.e. a card from each player) which contain Jacks, Queens, Kings, Aces and 2s, which are all valuable cards. In this game Ace is higher than a King and a 2 higher than an Ace.

Pip begins by the player to the left of the dealer leading. He puts a card face upwards on the table. Each player must follow suit if he can (i.e. put down a card of the same suit), with a more valuable card if possible. If he is unable to do so he can either discard an unwanted card or play a trump.

The trick is won by whoever plays the highest trump or (if none are played) the highest card in the leading card's suit. If two players play the same winning card the second one played is regarded as the winner. (Remember this can often happen because two packs are being used.) The winner of each trick keeps these cards apart from the rest.

As soon as one round has been played each player draws a card from the stack, thus restoring the number of his cards to seven. Any player who finds he now has a King and Queen of the same suit calls out 'Pip' and lays down the cards, face upwards, in front of him. For this success he scores fifty points, and the suit of the Royal couple becomes trumps for the next round. If no one calls 'Pip', trumps remain as in the previous round.

When there are not enough cards in the stack to go round, play continues until the cards in the players' hands are used up.

Each player keeps all the cards he wins in each trick. At the end of the game he goes through them to obtain his score. He earns eleven points for each 2, ten points for each Ace, five for each King, four for each Queen, and three for each Jack.

Rockaway

This is such a simple game that it is best played when very young brothers and sisters want to share in the fun. But there should be someone old enough to see fair play and to check the counting at the end.

Two packs of cards are required, well shuffled together. Each player (and there should be six or more, though you can play quite well with as few as four) receives seven cards from the dealer.

One card is placed in the centre of the table face upwards. Beside it goes the rest of the pack, face downwards.

The object of the game is to get rid of all the cards in one's hand. Play starts with the player on the left of the dealer. He can dispose of any card in his hand which is of the same suit or the same value as the exposed card.

For example, if the exposed card is the 4 of Clubs he can place on it any 4 or any Club in his hand. To make it even easier, any Ace can be played at any time, whether the exposed card is an Ace or not, and whatever the suit.

A player will be unlucky at the start if he has no card which meets one of these conditions, but if he cannot play he must draw from the top of the pack beside the exposed card until he picks up a playable card.

If the new card enables him to resume playing from the cards in his hand he does so. For instance, he may have had to draw from the pack because he had no Hearts, no 7, and no Ace to put on the exposed 7 of Hearts. Then he picks up the 3 of Hearts, which he plays. Then if he has a 3 of Clubs, Spades or Diamonds he can play it, and goes on in this way playing from his hand until he has no suitable card, whereupon the next player has his turn.

When there are no more cards in the stack, play continues with turns missed by anyone without a suitable card.

The player who first gets rid of all his cards is the winner. He, of course, has no score against him, The others make up their penalty score from the total of the pips on their unplayed cards, with Kings, Queens and Jacks counting eleven and an Ace (which it is very unwise to keep) a heavy penalty of fifteen.

Three games are usually enough for most players. The scores of each player in each game are added together, and the player with the lowest number of penalty points is the overall winner.

Whist

This is quite a difficult game. You need to have a good memory because you have to try to remember the value of all played cards, and at an early stage of the game work out from the way they are played the probable values of those still held by your two opponents and by your partner (whist is a game for four players, divided into two partnerships).

But don't be put off by this warning. Whist is simple enough to play without breaking the rules. The hard part is playing whist well, and that will come with practice. The best way is to ask three friends to join you in order to learn the game, at first keeping this page handy so you can all refer to it, and not trying too hard to win. For a few games you might even play with everyone seeing everyone else's cards, each player explaining why he is playing a particular card.

The rules are not numerous and are easily understood, so let's imagine you are actually sitting down at a small table, with your partner sitting opposite and the opposing partners on each side.

Each player draws a card from the pack. The lowest value decides who shall deal. All cards are dealt out, the dealer starting with the player on his left. The last card (which goes to the dealer) is shown to everyone, and its suit decides the trump suit (see p. 85) for the game.

The player to the left of the dealer starts by putting one card face up on the table. The object of the game is to take tricks (see p. 85) in cooperation with your partner. Each player in turn must put down a card and follow suit if he can. If he has no card of that suit he can play any card he wishes.

If the first card played is one of the trump suit, the highest trump card played by the four players wins the trick, and whoever put it down collects the trick. (One member of each partnership stacks the tricks they have won by his side.)

If the first card is not in the trump suit, then the highest card of the first card's suit wins, unless it is beaten by a card in the trump suit (whoever puts this down making sure first that he does not have a card of the leading card's suit).

The important thing in whist is to remember that you are not playing by yourself but with a partner. Therefore, if the second person to play is your partner, he has played a trump, and you have no card in the leading suit but a trump of greater value than his, you must consider carefully whether you should throw away (put down some small value card in another suit) and save your trump. The alternative is to play it in order to try to prevent the fourth player from beating your partner with a higher trump than his. This is where you need to think about the cards which have been played and the clues you have gained about your opponents' cards. In any event, the third player should never play a trump of a lower value than that already played by his partner, unless he is forced to near the end of the game when cards are running out.

The winner of a trick leads on the next round, playing whatever card he wishes, with the other players obeying the rules about following suit, throwing away, or playing a trump card as explained above.

Scoring is based on the number of tricks taken by each partnership. As there are thirteen tricks to be won and the score depends on the number of tricks won in excess of six, one side must win at least one point, taking seven tricks against the opponents' six tricks.

You may wonder what an experienced whist player means when he talks about points for Honours. It is not really necessary to worry about this while you are a beginner, and indeed many adult enthusiasts ignore Honours altogether.

When they are made part of the game, Honours points are awarded for the Ace, King, Queen and Jack of the trump suit. Partners who between them are dealt all four of these cards score four points; with three of them two points.

Honours bring a big slice of luck into the game. One side might get a poor score in tricks and still win because of the luck of getting Honours points.

There are no strict rules about the number of rounds to play, but most whist players regard seven points as ending a game, while three games are called a rubber. The partnership ends with a rubber, and players cut a stack of cards to decide a new partnership or in some other way make a change in the arrangement.

Party Games

Animal, Vegetable, Mineral

You probably know the 'twenty questions' game when players have to guess a word and are merely told that it is animal, vegetable or mineral. This game is different, and in some ways just as hard.

It is best played with two teams with at least three players in each. If they are very clever indeed there will be twenty-six battles, as someone manages to help his team survive from A at the start to Z at the end.

This is how you play. A tossed coin decides which team shall start. The captain of the winning side calls out A, adding the word Animal, Vegetable or Mineral and then the name of one of the challenged team. While his team counts in unison from one to ten the named player on the other side must name something starting with A, and in whatever category the challenger named.

For example 'A Animal' could be answered by Ass; 'A Vegetable' by Artichoke; 'A Mineral' by Aluminium.

If a correct answer is given within the time limit, the other team's captain calls out B and names the category. No answer or an incorrect one means that the challenging team retains the right to challenge on the next letter.

Two failures by a named member, and he must drop out of the game. But if you have only two or three members in each team it is better to make the penalty three failures.

No whispering or talking by a questioned player's teammates is allowed, but they can help by mime or pointing to a picture or object in the room.

Musical Chairs

Most people know the original version of this game. A row of chairs is placed side by side and facing in alternate directions, with one chair fewer than the number of players taking part. They walk in a circle round the row while music plays, and as soon as the music stops everyone must sit on a chair. The one unsuccessful player drops out, a chair is removed and the game continues until one person is left. Here are some variations of the game.

Instead of chairs the players walk round a circle of small counters on the floor, equal to the number of players, but with one counter a different size or colour from the rest. This counter is the penalty one. Whoever is unable to get near enough to pick up a winning counter but forced to take the penalty one when the music stops drops out.

After each round one person collects the counters, removing one but always keeping the penalty counter, and rearranges them in the same size of circle so that the counters are farther apart each time.

This counter version is good fun in the garden when a really large space can be used and it is not too easy to see a small object half hidden in the grass. In the garden game things can be made a little more difficult by ruling that everyone must run all the time, or hop round, or run backwards.

Another version of the game can be played either outdoors or indoors. Set out some chairs or other objects to mark the inner margin of a circular track. Everyone must move round outside these obstacles. Mark squares about one metre in size with chalk or sellotape next to any two of the chairs, on the outside of the circle. These are penalty areas and anyone with both feet or even part of a foot inside the square has to fall out when the music stops. When the number of players has decreased to three or four it is a good idea to remove one penalty area, so that only one player risks having to drop out each time. In this game players are not allowed to run.

For yet another version of the game you need to prepare some pieces of cardboard just large enough for a player to stand on. Make enough to have one per player and number them in large writing from 1 upwards. They are placed on the floor in as big a circle as possible and in any order, and the players walk round them.

Someone must supervise the game and operate the record player or radio. When the music stops each player must stand on a card. The organiser, without looking, then calls out a number. The player on this number falls out, taking his card with him. The organiser must, of course, keep a note of the numbers he calls so that he does not repeat them. Finally there will be only one player and one card left.

Underwater Bull's Eye

A novel party game for any number of players. Have someone as referee and prize giver. He will have to roll up one of his sleeves and have a towel handy.

All you need is a deep bowl or, better still, a large glass water jug. The water should be at least twenty centimetres deep. Before filling the receptacle with water place a small coin or counter – the smaller the better – at the bottom and in the centre.

Give each player a few coins or counters, not much larger than the one in the water, and they then take turns at dropping them into the water, trying to cover the target coin. The coin must be dropped from above the water. Anyone touching the water is out of the game.

A successful drop wins the player his own coin and any others which previously missed the target, the winnings being retrieved from the water by the referee.

It is much harder to hit the target coin than you might imagine, especially with lightweight plastic counters.

General Post

A well-tried party favourite, which is really a better version of blind man's buff.

An older person, not actually playing the game, is Postmaster. After all the players but one are sitting in a circle, with a clear space in the centre, he makes a list of the towns the players want to represent (the player not sitting in the circle, who is the postman, should also choose the name of a town as his turn will come later).

The postman is blindfold. He stands in the middle of the circle, at the same time all the players changing places in case the blindfold player has a good memory.

The postmaster calls out 'I have a letter going from London to Sydney' or whatever towns he likes to choose from the list. London and Sydney must then change places, with the blindfold postman trying to catch one of them as they dodge across the circle.

Now and then the postmaster calls 'General post!' and everyone must change places, but still evading capture.

If the postman manages to capture a moving player he exchanges places with him and the game continues with a new postman, but he can also achieve success by sitting on one of the chairs vacated by the moving players. Of course his big opportunity to do this is during general post.

Rhyming I Spy

Try this version as a change from the usual 'I Spy' game. In the original game one player has to guess which object the other one is thinking of when he says: 'I spy with my little eye something beginning with . . .' giving the initial letter of the object as a clue.

In the rhyming version, if your selected object is 'wall', for example, you could say: 'I spy something rhyming with ball' (or hall, Paul, stall, trawl). That would be easy even for very young players, but with some ingenuity and longer words, changing your call to 'I spy something with an ending rhyming with . . .' the game becomes more of a challenge, especially if you are limited to three guesses or (when more than two are playing) one guess each.

For example, what word could be intended with an end rhyming with face to race or pace? It might be bookcase, fireplace, or staircase. And what word could be intended with the end rhyme of net? The choice could be from carpet, pelmet, cigarette, teaset, packet, puppet, and so on.

Imitations

A party game which gets everyone playing, with no winners and no losers. Someone with plenty of bright ideas is leader, and everyone else lines up behind him.

The leader marches off, rapidly changing his movements, for example to a hop, a few paces on all fours, turning round and walking backwards, hands in the air, sitting down for a moment, jumping forward with feet together, and so on.

The player behind must imitate the leader's movement

as soon as he sees it, the player behind him doing the same, and so on right down the line. If there are ten or more in the line the leader will have started a new movement before the last player has imitated the previous one.

When parents allow it the line should move from room to room, under tables, round chairs, and in any place to make the imitation trip a novelty, possibly going out of doors too.

O'Grady

This party game is usually intended for the juniors, but don't think that you are ever to old to lose, since even teenagers find themselves being beaten by six-year-olds. Anyway, the game needs a quick-thinking older person to issue the commands, and can be played indoors or outdoors.

The players stand in a circle, the bigger the better, and the commander stands in the centre. He issues a stream of orders, but they are to be obeyed only if they come from the mysterious Mr O'Grady. Without the words 'O'Grady says . . .' before the order, the players must ignore it.

The spokesman for O'Grady should make his orders as varied and amusing as he can, and mix up those to be obeyed with those to be ignored. For example he might give orders like these: 'O'Grady says start walking to the left' – 'Halt' – 'Start running' – 'O'Grady says turn round and go the other way' – 'O'Grady says jump' – 'Hands above heads' – O'Grady says sit down – 'O'Grady says lie flat' – 'Raise one leg in the air' – O'Grady says stand up '– 'Sit down' – 'O'Grady says call out your name'. There are many, many more orders you can devise.

Anyone who fails to obey an O'Grady order, or (and this is where the mistakes usually happen) obeys an order that should be ignored, drops out of the circle.

Up Jenkins

All that is needed for this game is a small coin. Players sit round a table, as close to one another as possible. One player is chosen as the finder and stands away from the table, the others moving their chairs to fill the gap.

While the finder closes his eyes and counts up to ten the coin is grabbed from the centre of the table by anyone quick enough to reach it. Then everyone's hands are placed below the table and the finder opens his eyes. With much shifting of arms, and misleading movements and expressions, the coin is passed under the table from one player to his neighbour, to and fro as considered most misleading to the finder.

When the finder believes that he knows who is holding the coin he touches the player on the shoulder and says 'Up Jenkins'. The player thus challenged must raise his clenched hands above his head.

The finder may feel certain that the coin is in one of the clenched fists and will then touch it. If the coin is in that hand he scores three points and has another turn as finder.

But if he is not absolutely sure, he does not touch the player but instead gives the order 'Down Jenkins'. The player lowers his arms until his clenched fists are on the table, and then straightens his fingers, palms downward.

Often there is the slight sound of the coin touching the table or it may momentarily be visible. In any event the finder can then touch one of the hands. If the coin was concealed by the hand he earns two points and has another turn.

Perhaps the finder is still not quite certain, after his two orders of 'Up Jenkins' and 'Down Jenkins'. Without touching the player he makes one more demand: 'Open the window'.

The player, who has already placed his hands with fingers stretched and palms downwards on the table, must then spread his fingers apart.

If the coin was held between two fingers it will then become visible, but possibly, if he is clever, he has managed to conceal it under one of his palms. Even if he is still doubtful, the finder must now touch one of the hands. If he is right, he gets one point and another turn.

If the finder fails after any of the three attempts, or if he challenges someone who does not have the coin, he changes places with the player he challenged.

Up Jenkins can be played as a team game, with the players divided equally and sitting on opposite sides of the table. One team has the coin and the others watch until their captain shouts 'Up Jenkins', whereupon all the players opposite raise their clenched fists above their heads.

The finding team confers and comes to agreement on which player to challenge, points being awarded as in the free-for-all game. Right or wrong, each team has the coin alternately so that the chance to win points is equally shared.

Slap Penny

This game needs at least ten players, divided into two teams with five on each side. The two teams stand facing one another. A chair is arranged at each end of each row, and ten coins placed on one chair of each team. On the word 'go' the players beside the coins pick up one coin and place it on the hand nearest the chair, holding the hand and palm upwards.

The coin is then slapped from that palm to the other palm and then to the palm of the next player, who in turn transfers it to his other hand, and so on. The first player palms the other coins as quickly as his neighbour can take them on their journey.

A coin must never be clutched. If it is dropped, it is returned to the starting point on the chair.

The last player in the line drops the coins on to the chair set beside him. To make the game longer he can then start sending the coins back along the line in the same way, the first team to get all ten coins safely back to the starting chair being the winner.

This game sounds much easier than it is. The problem is transferring the coin from your own hand to your neighbour's without dropping it as you make an awkward twist of the wrist.

Who Am I?

This is another party game, and is best played as soon as all the guests have arrived. It will help them to get to know one another.

Cut up some small squares of paper, as many as the number of guests, and write on them the names of well known people – kings and queens in history, TV stars, pop singers, story book characters, and so on. The party's host fixes with a paper clip (or, if he can be careful, a pin) one name to the back of each guest, who then approaches the other to find out who he is.

The questioned player must answer only 'Yes', 'No' or 'Don't know', so the questions have to be carefully thought out, such as 'Am I a man?' 'Am I alive now?' 'Do I appear on TV?' 'Have you ever met me?' 'Am I a real person?' 'Am I a character in a story?'

If you want to make the game a competition you can give

three small prizes for the first, second and third guests who correctly identify the persons they are supposed to be.

Make sure, by the way, that there are no mirrors on the wall to tempt cheaters!

Puffball

For this party game guests are divided into two teams. The centre of the room, cleared of obstacles, is the track, and at one end is a chair or stool with enough space between the legs to pass a balloon underneath.

The teams gather side by side in two lines at the other end of the room, with the leading member of each team holding an inflated balloon.

On the word 'go' the players with the balloon go down on their knees, place their balloon at arm's length and then, on all fours, blow the balloon forwards towards the chair, through the chair legs, and back to the starting line, where the second member of the team is crouched on all fours ready to repeat the blowing process.

Apart from the fun on the up-and-back course there can often be big problems when both racers reach the chair at the same time. The balloon must not be deliberately touched, but you are allowed to bounce it off your opponent's body or limbs if it helps.

Puffball can be quite exhausting. The course should not be more than four or five metres in length.

Tricks and Stunts

Think of a Number

To work this mystifying thought-reading trick you will have to copy out the numbered squares shown in the sketches here. This will be quite a job but you will find it worthwhile when you challenge anyone to explain how you can quote whatever number he chooses from 1 to 60.

You ask your victim to think of a number under 61. Then one at a time you hand him the cards you have written, asking him if the selected number is on the card. Remember which cards yield the answer 'yes', or put them aside. Ignore the cards on which your victim says the chosen number does not appear.

Now act as if you were thought-reading, gazing closely at your victim's face and then studying the cards. While you are doing this add up the figures in the top right hand corner of the chosen cards. The total will give you the selected number.

Say your victim chooses 15 as the number. It appears on cards 1, 2, 4, and 5. The top right hand corner figures of these cards at $1+8+4+2 = 15$.

If you have ever watched a conjuror or thought-reader on TV or the stage, you may have noticed that now and then they pretend to fail to do what they promised the first time.

This is a good idea to suggest your thought-reading is very, very difficult.

When you go through the gazing and thinking routine pretend to be annoyed and worried, saying something like 'You are not concentrating on the number hard enough. I can't get your thought waves. Please think again.'

Then, of course, you correctly give the thought-of number.

Bing Bang Bong

Keep this game in mind next time you get bored on a long car or train journey. And you might even persuade your maths teacher to include it as a change from an ordinary lesson after exams or at the end of term.

The first player says 1, the next 2, and so on in turn, counting from 1 towards a target as high as you want. You will be super at multiplication if any of you reach 100 without a mistake, because here is the trick – you must say Bing for 3 or any multiple of it, Bang for 5 and its multiples and Bong for 7 and its multiples. Thus the first player says 1, the next player 2, but the third player says Bing. The fourth turn produces 4, the fifth Bang, the sixth Bing, and the seventh Bong.

Anyone failing to say the correct word is out. He is also out if he does not include all the possible words. Thus 15 (3 × 5) is Bing Bang, 21 (3 × 7) is Bing Bong. If you get far enough you will discover that 105 is Bing Bang Bong (3 × 35, 5 × 21, 7 × 15)!

Another version of this game, Buzz, can be played faster, as there is only one number, 7, to remember. But the catch is that 7, its multiples, and any number containing 7 (17, 27, 37, and so on) must be replaced by a nice loud buz-z-z-z, repeated according to the number of 7s involved. So 14 (2 × 7) is buzz-buzz, 21 (3 × 7) is buzz, buzz, buzz, and 27 is called out as twenty buzz. As in Bing Bang Bong, you must include all the alternatives.

The game gets very noisy after you reach 70! Think of two buzzes for 77 followed by eleven buzzes as the alternative version (11 × 7)!

On Guard

You can work out this problem by yourself and, after finding out how it is done, challenge a friend to do so. You need eight coins or counters – seven of the same size or colour and one different. This contrasting counter is the officer in charge of the sentries to be put on guard round a secret research station.

The sketch shows the plan of the station and the guard points. You may prefer to copy this on a larger scale. This is quite easy if you first draw the two sets of vertical and horizontal lines and then join up their points with four diagonals as shown.

The officer orders his men, one by one, to take up their posts, always starting from a vacant point and marching along a line to another vacant post. When the seven men are in position the officer takes up the remaining post himself.

Do you find it difficult? Actually it is very simple.

March the first guard from any point you like. Then march the next guard so that he ends up on the point from

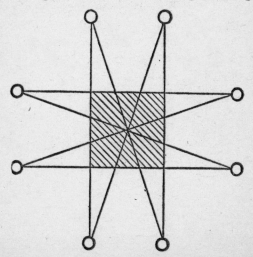

which the previous guard started. Continue with this method of ending on the point from which the previous guard started and you will be left with all seven guards in position, and one point left for the officer.

Message Square

If you take the trouble to copy out the large lettered square shown in the sketch, you can do a trick which so-called fortune tellers and soothsayers have been doing ever since writing was invented. The messages which the magic square provides are rather silly, but you may be sure that

everyone will be very impressed.

Copy out the square, being careful to get all the letters in the right order as shown, on as large a piece of paper or white cardboard as you can obtain, so the letters can be large and clear.

Ask your 'client' to think of a question he would like answered – something about his future fortunes. It adds to the interest if he writes the question on a piece of paper to show to anyone else watching, but he must not tell you what it is.

Next you ask him to place his finger on any letter he likes on the square. You then tell him to write down the letters you call out.

You start with the selected letter, and then call out every fifth letter after it, moving from left to right, line by line, and shifting to the top of the card after the letters in the last line have been dealt with.

The important thing for you to do is to memorise the first letter which you called out from the top line, for this is the starting letter of the message.

Let's imagine that the chosen letter is N in the third line. Counting from left to right every fifth letter after N is D A T T A I N T H Y W I S H W A I T A.

That gives a strange word NDATTAINTHYWISH-WAITA. If you start with the first letter from the top line, W, which appears fifth from the end, you get a message 'Wait and attain thy wish'. This does not mean much but is almost certain to make sense whatever the question was. For instance, 'Shall I play in the school football team?' or 'Will I get some money for my birthday?' are both satis-factorily answered.

If you want to discover all the messages contained in this square, for your private information, count the fifth letter from any spot you wish and decode the message by starting the words from the first letter chosen in the top row.

Find His Age

The thought-reading stunt explained on page 102 can, of course, be used to discover someone's age if you ask him to select the cards which include that figure. But as you probably know your friend's age anyway, he will not be very impressed.

This trick, however, is bound to baffle him. Both of you must be fairly good at arithmetic as quite a lot of adding, subtracting and multiplying is involved. But the effort is worth it, for you will not only be able to tell your friend his age, but also his birth month.

First, tell your friend to write down the number of the month in which he was born. Then say to him: 'Double this number. Add 5. Multiply by 50. Add your age last birthday. Subtract 365. Add 115. Now tell me the result.'

If the result has only two figures, the first will be the birth month and the second his age. With three figures, the first will be the month, and the last two his age. With four figures, the first two are the month and the last two his age.

As an example, say your friend is twelve and was born in May (the fifth month of the year). Under your instructions, he writes down the following:

His birth month   5
Multiplied by 2   10
Plus 5   15
Multiplied by 50   750
Plus his age (12) 762
Minus 365   397
Plus 115   512 (Birth month 5 – May – and age 12)

If you and your friend are not too clever at arithmetic, here is a simpler age-finding trick. Tell your friend to think of his age, multiply it by 3, add 6, and divide by 3, giving you the answer. You then deduct 2, and the result is your friend's age.

For instance, your friend's age is 10

Multiplied by 3   = 30
Plus 6   = 36
Divided by 3   = 12
Minus 2   = 10

Match Games

A nice thing about these match games is that you, with special knowledge, can be sure to win every time, though there is always a chance that your opponent may have read this book too and know how the tricks work!

Take twenty-one matches. Be sure that either they are used or they are the safety kind (or you can play the game with counters or coins). Place them on the table in neat rows. The number of rows and number of matches in each row do not matter, but neatness will help you to note how many matches are removed, and this is essential if you are to win.

Challenge your opponent to take turns with you at removing one, two or three matches, with the object of leaving one match for the last turn. The player who has to take this last match is the loser.

If you can politely persuade your opponent to start the game, carefully note how many he takes, and then on your turn take a match or matches to make the number up to four. If your opponent takes one you take three; if he takes two you take two; if he takes three you take one. Keep to the four rule on every turn, and you will find that he is always left with the last match.

Perhaps your opponent is rather suspicious about the way you eagerly invite him to start the game, and refuses to do so. Don't worry, you can still win. Just count the number of matches taken and take the fourth, eighth, twelfth, and sixteenth match yourself. Thus if at the start your opponent takes three, you take one; if he takes two, you also take two.

After you have taken the sixteenth match continue playing as explained for the first method, making the number up to four matches whatever your opponent takes. After the sixteenth has been taken by you there are only five matches left, so if your opponent takes three, there are two left and you take one, leaving the last match for him. If he takes two, you take two. If he takes one, you take three. So you can't lose.

Another version of the same battle of wits requires sixteen matches. Arrange them in four rows with seven in the top row, five in the second, three in the third and one in the bottom row.

In this game it is vital somehow to persuade your opponent to start first if you want to be certain of winning.

The object, as before, is to leave one match to be picked up, making that the losing turn. The only rule is that however many matches are picked up on each turn, they must all come from the same row. You can pick up any number of matches at once.

You will find there are several ways of winning if you start first, but they will not be easy to discover without a lot of practice. One winning series is as follows:

Your opponent takes three matches from the second row (leaving two).

You take seven from the top row (leaving none).

He takes two from the second row (leaving none).

You take three from the third row (leaving none).

He has to pick up the only match left, in the bottom row.

Physical Feats

These stunts require dexterity and suppleness more than great strength, so they are not too difficult for anyone challenging an older friend. But one or two are impossible, however old and strong you are, even if they sound simple!

Hold a coin in your hand. Stand on an agreed line marked by the design on a carpet or by the edge of a rug. Bend down without letting your knees touch the floor and place the coin as far forward as possible, using your other hand to support yourself. Then, without moving your feet, return to an erect position in one movement, at the same time taking your supporting hand from the floor. Measure the distance of the coin from the standing line and see who can beat the distance with his coin.

Get a bamboo cane about 1·5 metres long. Hold it across behind your back with the palms of your hands facing forwards. You can position your hands as far apart as you wish. Lift the bamboo over your head, without leaving go with either hand, and bring it down in front of your knees. Lift one leg (your right will be easiest if you are right-handed) round your arm on that side and then through the stick. Still firmly gripping the stick, pass your other hand over your head and back, stepping out of the stick. If you find this stunt very difficult with a bamboo try it first with a piece of string.

Take a small sweet in one hand. Crouch down, knees on the floor and arms bent so that your elbows touch your knees. Place your hands close together, palms downwards, with the sweet freed from your grip and on the floor below one hand. Now clasp your hands behind your back and try to bend down and pick up the sweet with your mouth, without over-balancing.

Stand sideways with one shoulder and foot touching a wall, hands straight down beside your body so the arm also touches the wall. Now move the leg farther from the wall sideways, forwards or backwards without moving the foot you are standing on. Give these instructions to a friend, but don't boast that you will do the stunt yourself. It's impossible!

Here's another one which can't be done. Bend your fingers and press both hands together so that the knuckles are touching, and the palms are facing towards your body. Now raise the third finger (the ring finger) of each hand and try to make the tips touch. You must not move the other finger or your hands.

Tell the biggest and strongest friend you know that you can prevent him moving with just one of your fingers. Ask him to sit on a hard kitchen-type chair, feet extended, arms folded on his chest, and head tilted over the top of the chairback so that he is looking at the ceiling. Place the tip of one of your fingers firmly on the centre of your victim's forehead and then challenge him to get off the chair without uncrossing his arms or bending his legs. As long as his head remains under the slight pressure of your finger he will not be able to get up.

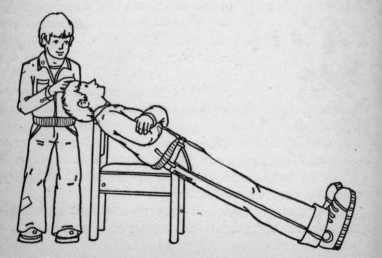

Word and Paper Games

Boxes

A game for a dull day when you feel like sitting quietly for a time. It is best played by two, but three or four can play, though it becomes very hard when each player has to battle against more than one opponent.

Take a piece of ruled paper from an exercise book and mark eleven lines with dots down the left-hand side. Mark ten dots along the top line next to the first, at the same distance apart as the ruled lines. Now you have quite a lot of preparation to do, for the dots have to be repeated on each line downwards so that you have dots marking the corners of a hundred squares – ten down and ten across.

Each player joins up two dots on each turn, the object being to complete a box with the fourth line where three already exist. The player completing a box has an extra turn in drawing a further line. Sometimes this new line will complete another box, and then he has yet another turn.

The player puts the initial of his name inside each box he completes – J when Jennifer completes a box, P when Philip gets one, for example.

It sounds a very simple game, but as more and more lines are drawn you will find it quite difficult to avoid drawing a line on a third side of a square and thus giving your opponent a chance to make a box.

Count up the initialled boxes at the end. The player with the most is the winner.

Hangman

This game originated in the bad old days when wrong-doers were executed even for such crimes as stealing a sheep. But it is such an attractive, thought-provoking game that it has long outlasted the cruel punishment on which it was based.

Unlike children of a couple of centuries ago, you may not know what a gibbet looks like, except from illustrations in story books about the past. The illustration shows a gibbet with its victim.

You will see that it is made up from a post, a wooden arm, a rope, the victim's head, body, two arms, and two legs. These make a total of nine items, and so there are nine chances to 'hang' your opponent when you challenge him – or to be hanged yourself when challenged.

Think of a word, and at the bottom of a piece of paper write a row of Xs equal to the number of letters it contains (The more vowels in it, the harder will it be for your opponent to guess what it is.)

Your opponent names a letter. If it is included in the word you write it down above the X or Xs in the appropriate positions.

If the letter is not in the chosen word you begin to construct the gibbet; after that is built with a wrong guess each for the post, arm, and rope, you add the body, one part at a time for each incorrect guess: first the head, then the body, an arm, another arm, a leg, and finally another leg for each wrong guess. The game then stops and you, as challenger, have won.

If your opponent completes the letters of the word before he is hanged, or at one stage makes a correct guess at the word, you have lost. If his guess is wrong another part is drawn.

You will find that the game is more interesting when more

than two people play – one challenging all the others at each turn. The fact that the guessers each have their own idea of what the word may be (they must not confer during the game) will result in a delay in the team solving the puzzle.

Syllable Chains

A sit-down game for two or more players. The first player says a two-syllable word. The second player takes the second syllable of that word and adds another syllable to make a new word. The next player does the same, and so on, turn by turn.

Anyone failing to give a word drops out. Eventually one player is left as the winner.

As an example of play, words might be: Enlist – Listen – Tender – Derail – Railway – Wayward – Warder – Derrick – Rickshaw.

This is quite a difficult game, and unless you are very good at English it helps to have a dictionary, with the other players counting up to twenty while the searcher tries to find an appropriate word. If he fails to find one in time he drops out.

Beetle

This is a well-tried party favourite. Each player is given a piece of paper and a pencil. You also need two dice. The players sit round the table and throw the two dice in turn.

The beetle is drawn bit by bit – an oval for the body, a small circle for the head, six legs on the sides of the body, and two feelers sprouting out of its head.

The body must be drawn first, and to do this the player must throw 6. He can draw a head for a 5, a feeler for 4, and a leg for 3. He must of course, have drawn the head before he can attach feelers. The first player to complete his beetle is the winner.

If you want to prolong the game make a rule that the total of the two dice is your number on each throw. But if you prefer to make it easier and quicker allow a choice – to take the total of the two dice or each separately. In the latter case a 3 and a 1 can be taken as a 3 for a leg or 4 for a feeler, and so on.

Giant Noughts and Crosses

You doubtless know how to play noughts and crosses, and you probably also know that whoever starts in the centre square cannot lose unless he makes a mistake. That is one reason why noughts and crosses can soon get boring.

But the Japanese have invented a much better version, using as many squares as you can bother to draw (and have the time to play)! For a start, try playing on a square made with fourteen vertical and fourteen horizontal lines, giving thirteen squares on each line across and down.

The object is to get five Os or five Xs in a straight line,

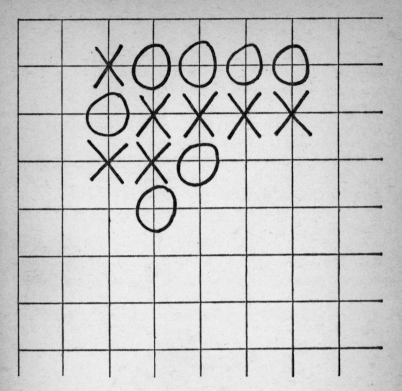

vertically, horizontally or diagonally.

A big difference from noughts and crosses is that the marks are made on the point where the lines cross, and not inside the squares.

The sketch shows how to draw the square, with an example of play after a few turns. As the square begins to fill up it becomes very difficult to prevent your opponent getting five in a line while planning your own tactics.

Draw a thick line with a coloured ballpoint through each success so that you can count your victories at the end of the game.

Noughts or crosses which have formed a line of five can still form part of another scoring line which crosses it.

Naval Battle

As you may know, when modern sea battles have occurred ships are often out of sight of one another, relying on radar and aircraft spotters to locate their targets. In this mock battle the ships on each side are hidden, so the battle plan you draw up on a sheet of paper must be screened from your opponent. This is a game for two players.

Draw an identical arrangement of squares on two sheets of paper – as many as you like, but eight squares across and ten squares down will give you a fairly long battle without too much risk of either side destroying all the enemy ships or losing all of their own.

Write the numbers 1 to 8 along the top of the plans, each number over a square, and the letters A to J down the side in the same way, so that every square on the plans has a reference number (for example 1A, 6B, 8J).

Each player, carefully concealing what he is doing, now arranges his ships on his squares. He has ten ships and they can be marked in any square he wishes. Use letters for the ships – A, B, C and so on.

Every ship has ten shells for the battle. Each player keeps a list of how much ammunition his individual ships have spent during the game. For example, he writes down A and alongside it, at the start of the game, the figure 10 (or ten strokes). During the game he must record his expenditure of shells, changing 10 to 9 or putting a line through one of the strokes.

It does not matter which ship is supposed to have fired a shell, though of course it cannot fire any remaining shells if it is hit during the game. The commander must watch that he has not run out of shells, when he would have to admit defeat through lack of ammunition.

All this may sound complicated, but will be simple and clear when you are actually fighting your battle. Each player

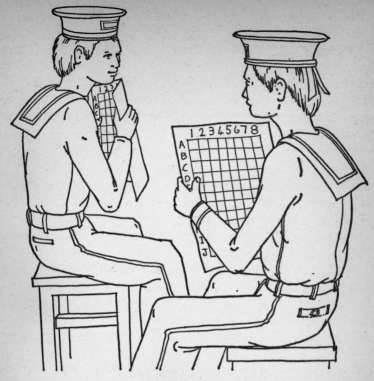

in turn decides which of his ships is going to fire a shell, and deducts one round of ammunition from that ship's store. He then chooses a square to fire at and calls out its number. The other player looks up the square on his chart. If it is empty he calls out 'Miss'. If it has a ship on it he calls out 'Hit', and when this happens that ship goes out of action for the rest of the game and its supply of ammunition is useless.

You write H for Hit and M for Miss on your battle map when you fire at the enemy, thereby avoiding firing into the same square later in the battle. You also know how many ships you have sunk and how many are still to be hit.

The commander who first loses all his ships or runs out of ammunition is the loser. If both sides run out of ammunition the commander with the most ships intact is the winner.

Crossword Sums

Draw a blank crossword square for each player with five squares across and five down. As in other games needing this kind of diagram, using ruled paper makes drawing the squares quick and easy. Each player should hold his square on a book or stiff card so that he can tilt it away from the prying eyes of his neighbour.

The first player calls out a letter. Everyone must use this letter, placing it wherever he wishes in the square. The object is to make up words, across from left to right and down. No plurals ending in 's' are allowed, and no proper nouns. Players call out a letter in turn.

When twenty-five letters have been called out and written into the squares, thus filling them, each player marks his score against each line on the right hand side and along the bottom.

Two-letter words do not score. Three-letter words score 1, four-letter words 5, and five-letter words 10.

There can be only one scoring word in each line. Thus 'Party' scores 10, but there cannot be an additional score of 5 for 'Part' or a third score of 1 for 'Art'.

Paper Football

All you need for this game is a pack of playing cards and a sheet of stiff paper or white cardboard about thirty centimetres long and fifteen wide. With a ball point pen or pencil mark the sheet into squares – eleven across and five down.

Mark the centre of the field with a large blob, and thicken the lines on the sides of the centre square at each end to indicate the goals.

With a coin or counter placed on the centre blob play can begin. Place the pack of cards face down within reach

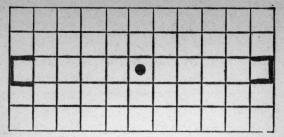

of the players (if there are more than two they form teams and play in turn).

One team is named black and the other red. Players take turns to pick up a card from the top of the pack. If a player picks up his team colour he can 'kick the ball'. If a card is not of his colour he misses the chance to play that time. Each card, used or not, is placed face downwards alongside the pack.

The first player to turn up a card of any value in his team colour moves the ball into a square adjacent to the centre blob. Normally he would, of course, move towards the opponent's goal, but there is nothing to stop him moving the ball in the other direction if he is working out a clever subsequent move.

After the first move to get the ball in play the value of the cards turned up becomes important. Ace to Five allows a move of one square, forwards, backwards, or sideways (but not diagonally). Six to Ten permits a move of two squares, which can be in a straight line or the first in one direction and the second at right angles to it. A Court card allows a move through three squares, again in a straight line, or through one or two right angles.

A goal is scored when the ball goes beyond the edge of the field between the thick lines marking the goal. The winner of a goal gets the first turn when play is resumed, with the coin back on the centre spot.

When the whole pack has been turned over the cards are shuffled and placed face downwards for further drawing.

Go-Go-Go

A nice game for an indoors day. Take a sheet of paper and rule it into squares – nineteen across and twenty-one down. (If you use ruled paper you will only need to draw the vertical lines.)

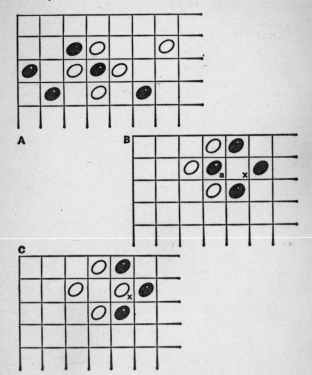

You need lots of counters in two contrasting colours, or you can use dried peas, haricot beans, coffee beans, or small pieces of coloured cardboard roughly cut into small squares.

Each player has one colour, and in turn places one of his counters on any square he likes, the object being to imprison the opponent's counter in a diagonal square as shown in sketch A. The trapped counter is then removed. On each turn a counter already in play may be moved, or a new one brought into play. A move by a counter already in play is made one square diagonally.

The game ends when one player has deployed all his counters so that it is useless for his opponent to play another counter as it will only be imprisoned by the next move.

There is only one important rule, needed to prevent a situation where one counter after another is imprisoned in the same place. It occurs when the counters have reached a position as shown in sketch B.

A study of the sketch will show that the player with white counters, if his is the next turn to play, can place his counter in space x and then remove the black counter a.

Then the player with black counters would play into the square previously occupied by his black counter a, thus capturing the white counter in space x. (See sketch C.) This capture by a counter only to be captured on the next move would continue for as long as the players had counters, and would be silly.

To prevent this happening there is the rule that when this position is reached the player whose counter first surrounds his opponent's counter cannot have his counter captured while it remains in its original position.

It may sound complicated, but in actual play you will find it quite simple.

Nine Men's Morris

This is a very old game for two players, and has been popular since the fourteenth century, when no doubt the Black Prince's soldiers played it when resting after their battles with the French. An attractive thing about this game is that you can play it indoors on a diagram drawn on paper or out of doors, drawing the plan in chalk on a hard surface or marking the points with small pieces of wood knocked into a grassy area. In the latter case players must remember that there are imaginary lines joining all the points, and none of them is a diagonal.

Each player has nine men – which can be coloured counters, pieces of cardboard, coins (when played indoors), stones – anything as long as one set of nine men is easily identified from the other.

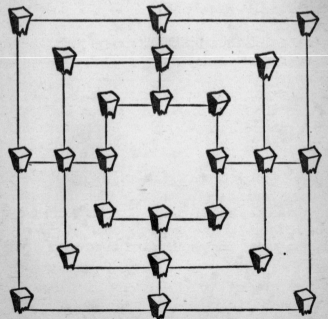

The illustration shows how the design should be drawn. Each side of the three squares has a base in the middle and one at each end, making eight for each square and twenty-four in all.

The object of the game is to get three men in line, down or across but not diagonally. Each player in turn places a new man on the design or moves one already in play to a vacant and adjacent base along the line (remember, not diagonally). When a player makes a line of three men, he can immediately remove any one of his opponent's men, and this is known as 'pounding'.

Eventually one player will have only three men left in play. But all is not lost, for he can then move to any vacant base he likes, ignoring the lines and the rule about not moving diagonally.

His opponent, who probably still has more than three men in play, must continue to observe the rules until he is also reduced to three, when he can also move where he likes.

Once a player is reduced to two men he has, of course, lost and the game ends.

More Beaver Books

We hope you have enjoyed this Beaver Book. Here are some of the other titles:

What's the Answer? A mixed bag of puzzles using numbers, words and pictures and all fun to try

Pleasure Trove A collection of stories, poems, limericks, jokes, riddles and things to make and do by Jennifer Curry

Picture Puzzles Ninety-six pages packed with a variety of brain-teasers, including mazes, 'spot-the-difference' and 'I spy' games, written and illustrated by Walter Shepherd

Tales told near a Crocodile Humphrey Harman has lived and worked for half a lifetime near Lake Victoria, the setting for these stories of African magic, legend and adventure. An evocative and fascinating collection of folk tales; with illustrations

Animal Quiz Johnny Morris, universally known and loved for his television programme *Animal Magic*, has created a picture quiz book about all sorts of animals, fish and birds, full of fun and fact for all the family

Twelve Great Black Cats and Other Eerie Scottish Tales. Ten weird and ghostly stories with a Scottish setting; by Sorche Nic Leodhas

New Beavers are published every month and if you would like the *Beaver Bulletin* – which gives all the details – please send a large stamped addressed envelope to:

Beaver Bulletin
The Hamlyn Group
Astronaut House
Feltham
Middlesex TW14 9AR

340333